I0476682

County of Kent Colouring Book for Kids!

(And Adults...)

Canterbury Cathedral

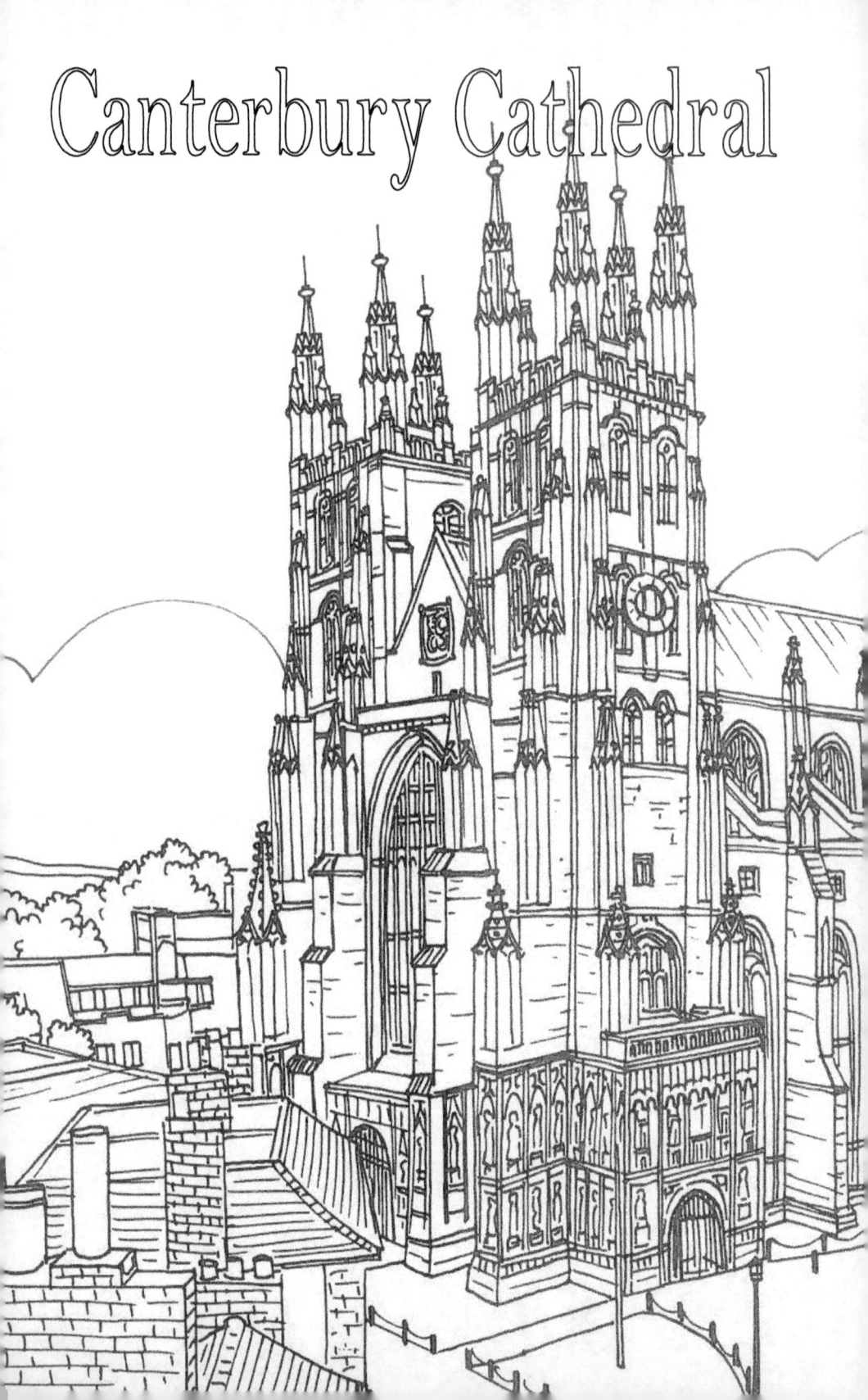

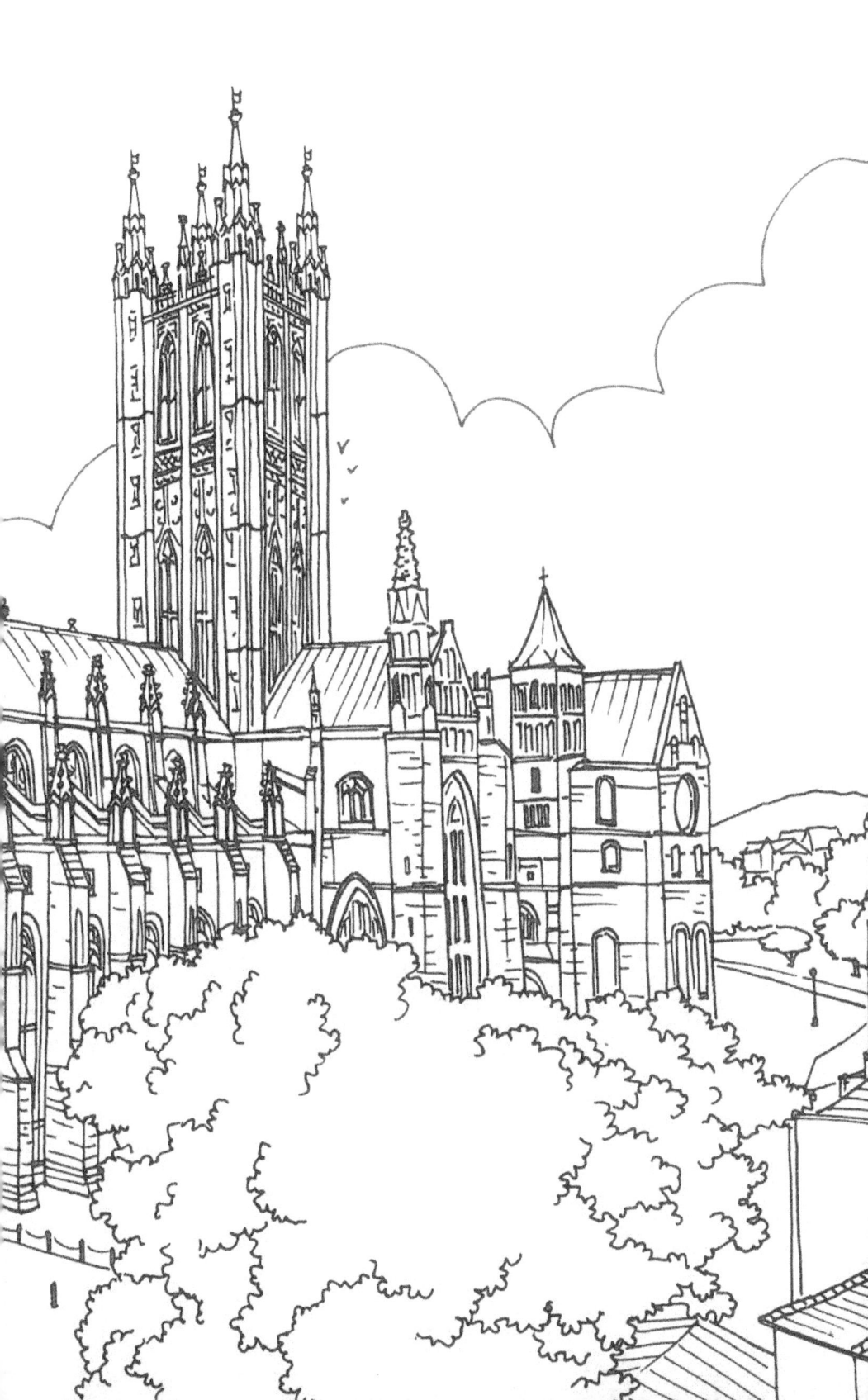

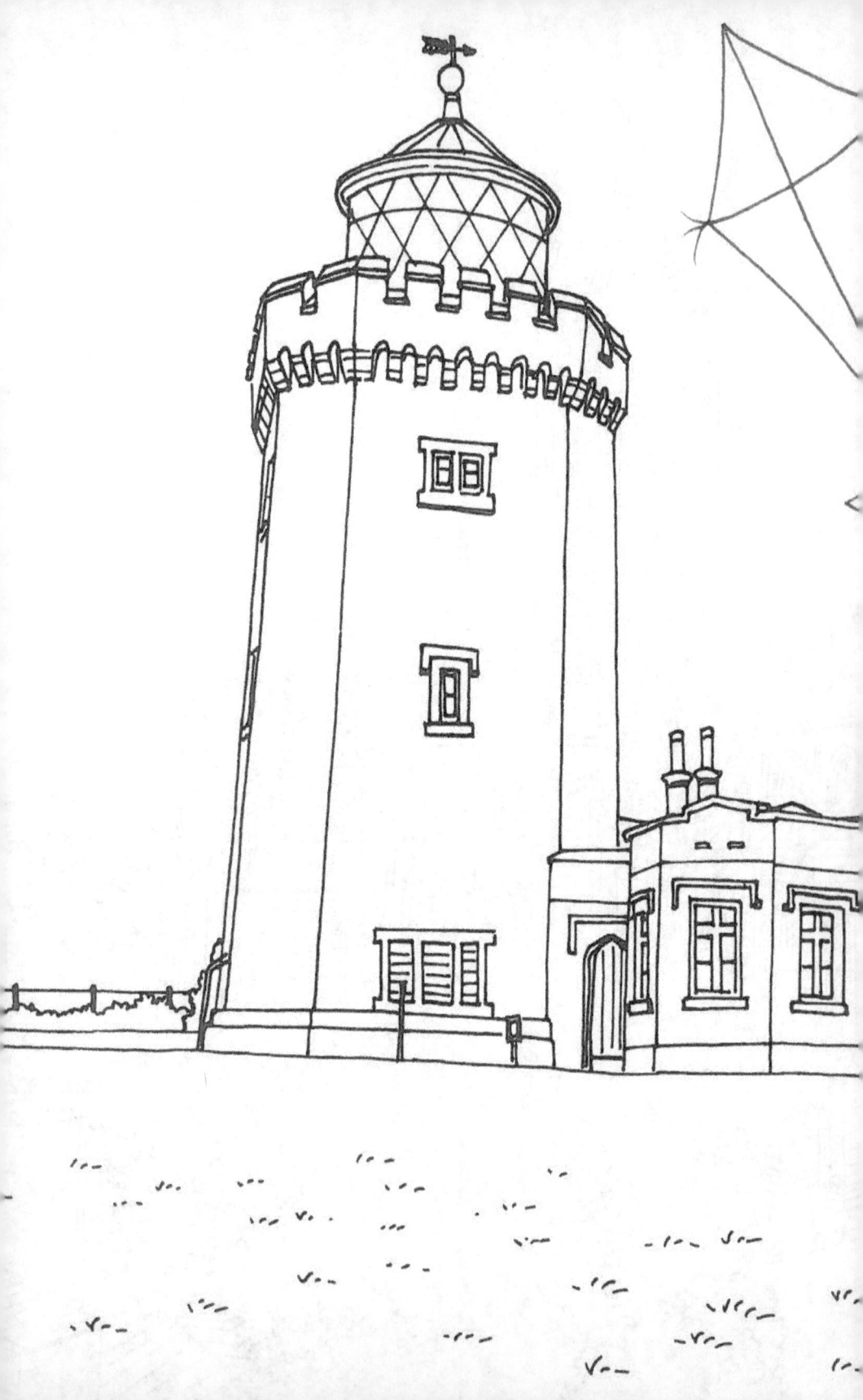

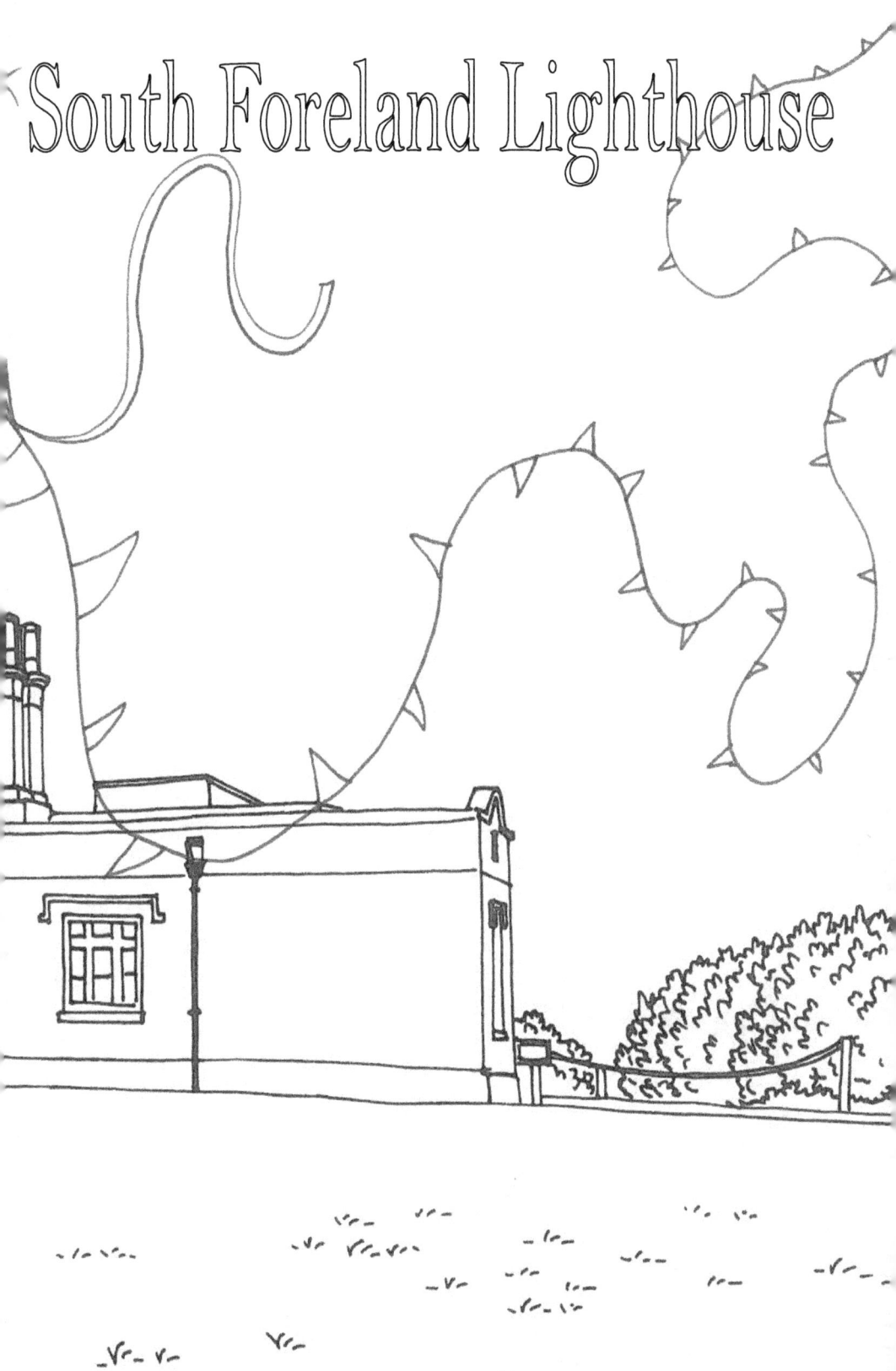

South Foreland Lighthouse

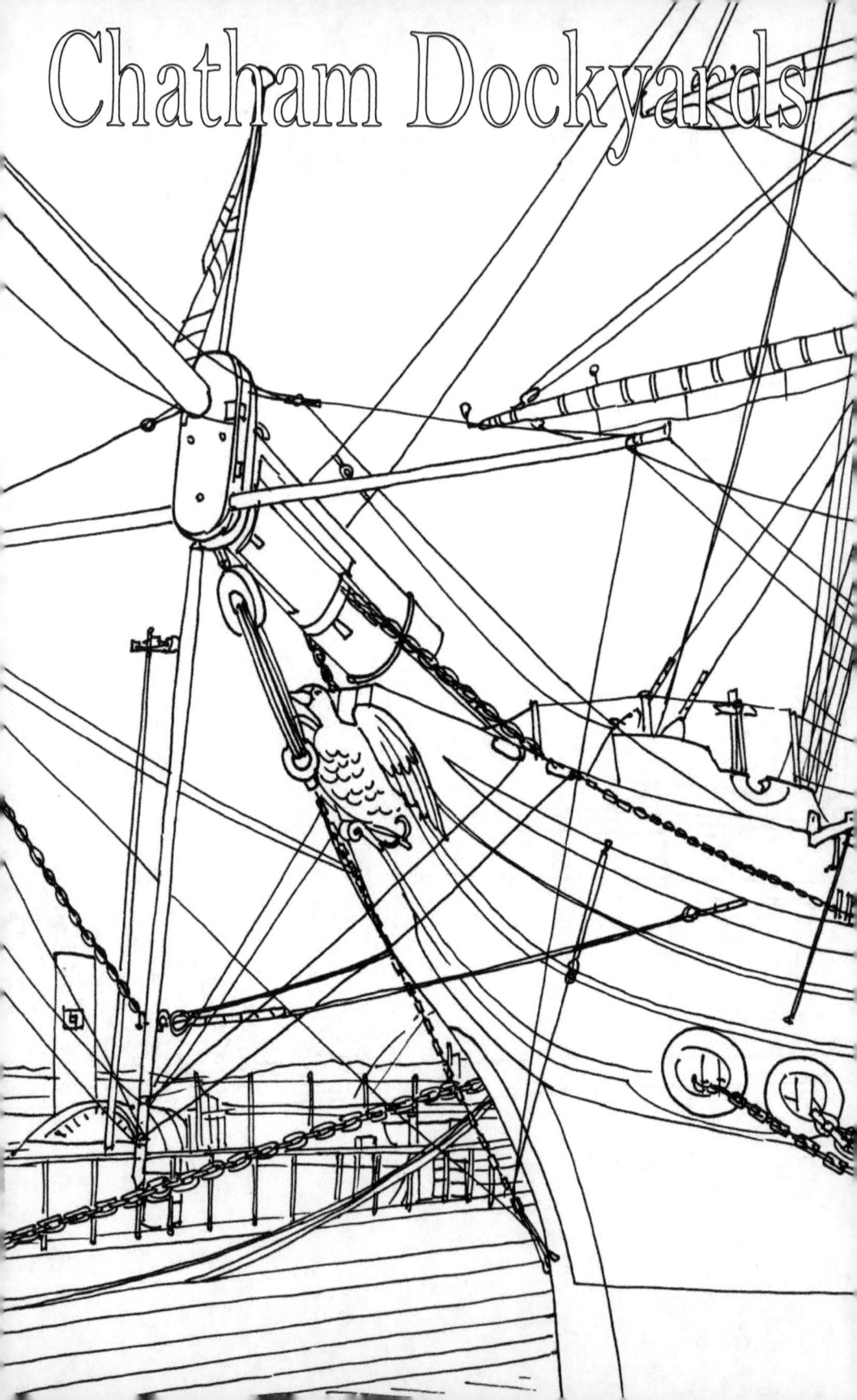

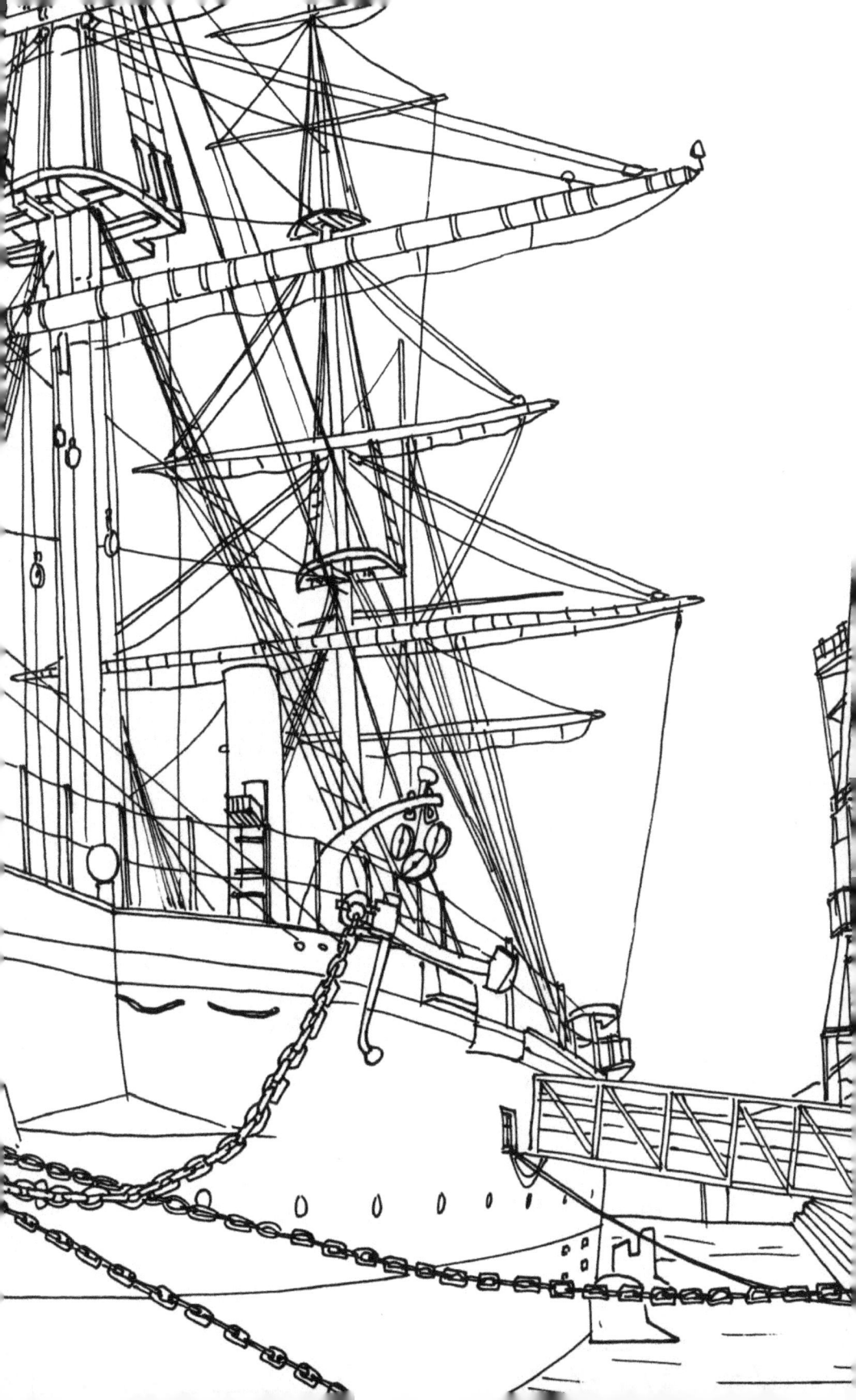

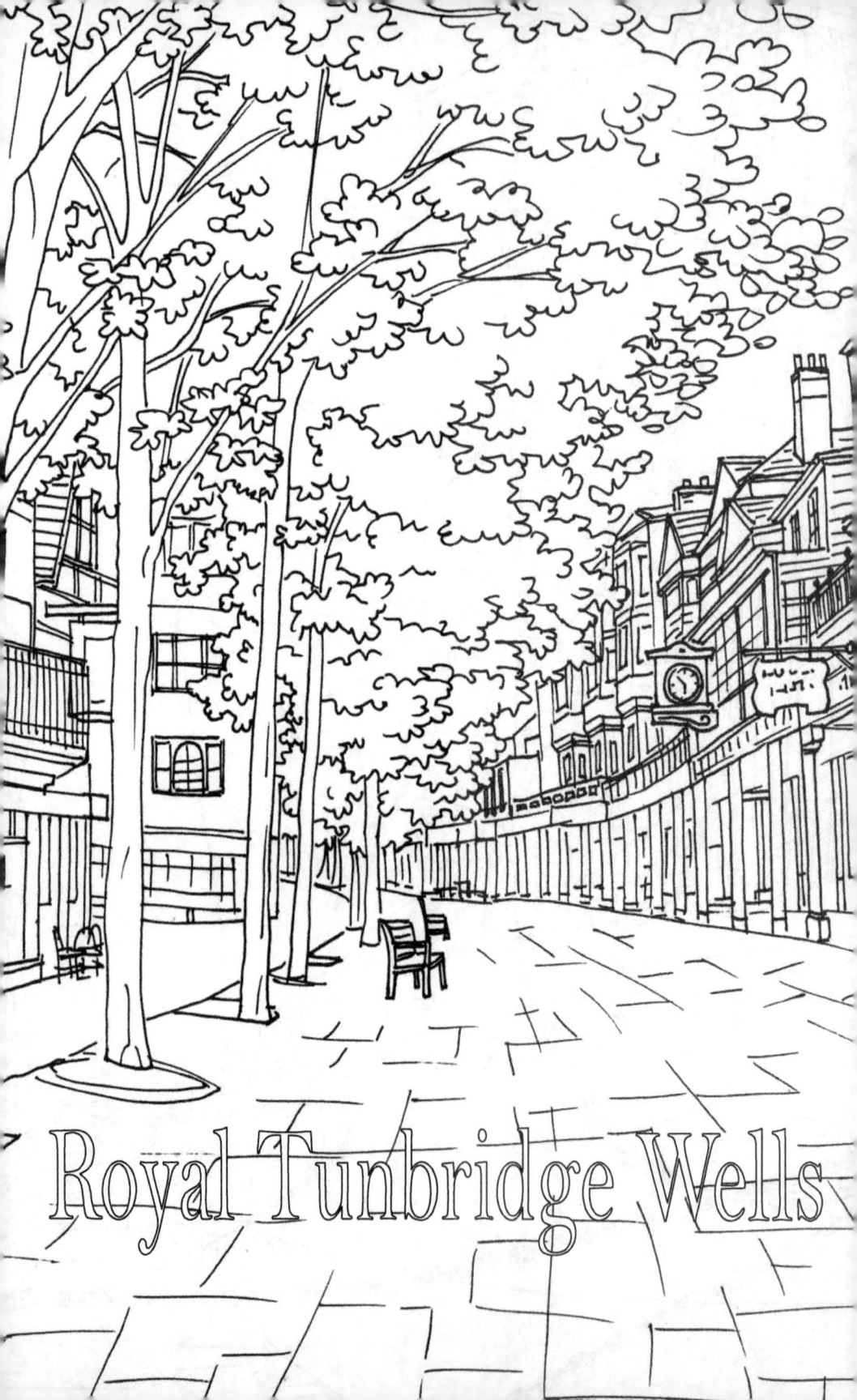

Royal Tunbridge Wells

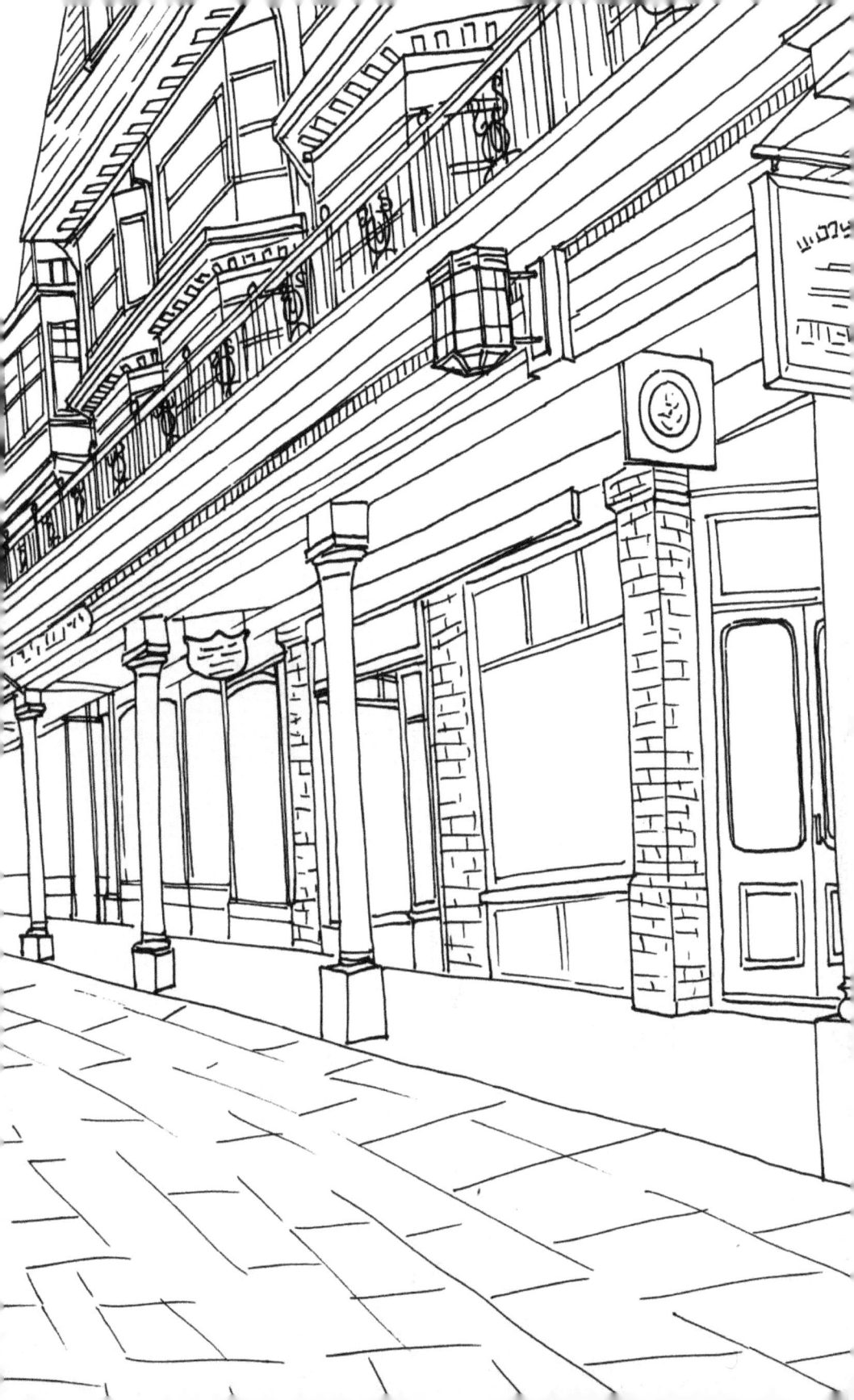

Tenterden

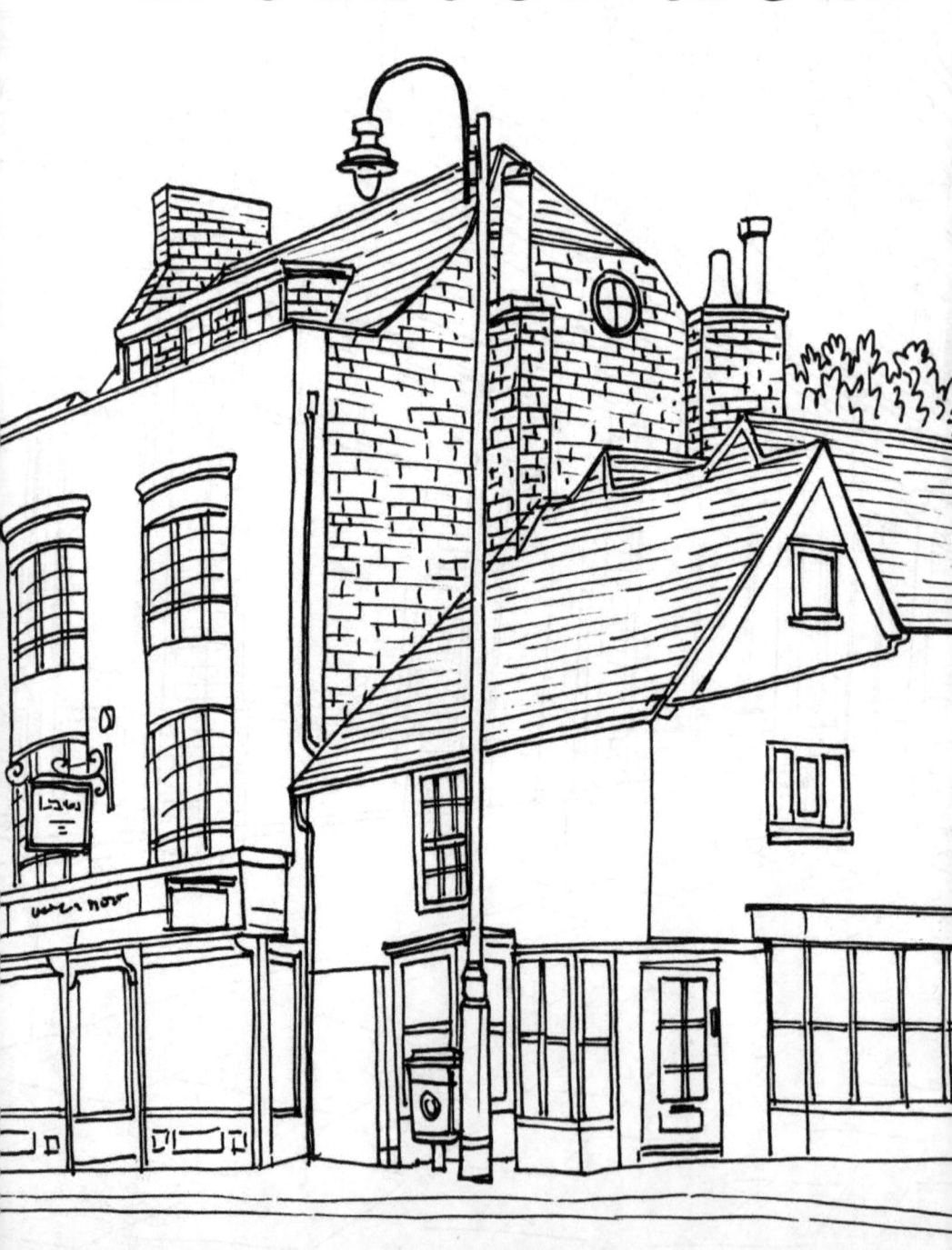

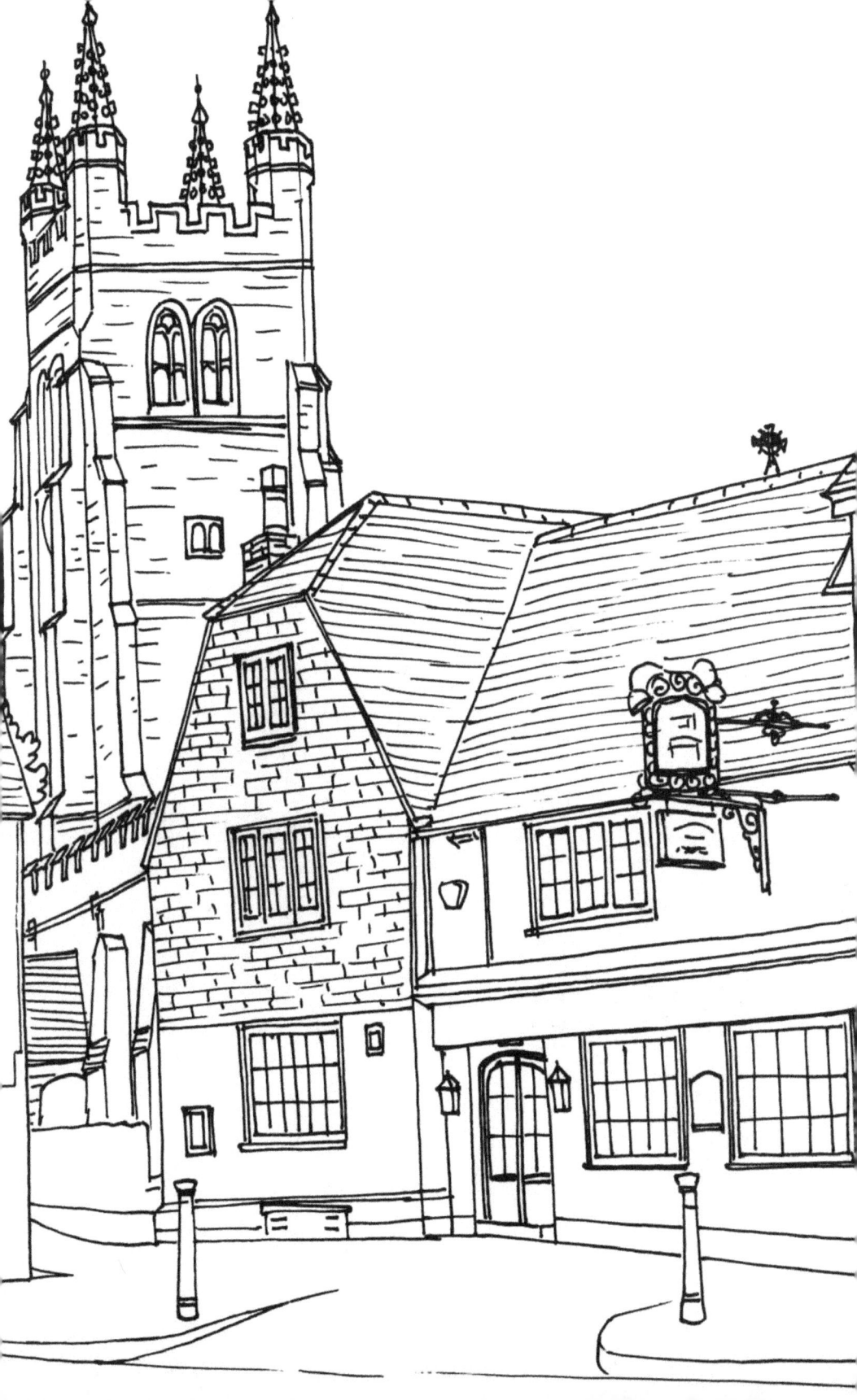

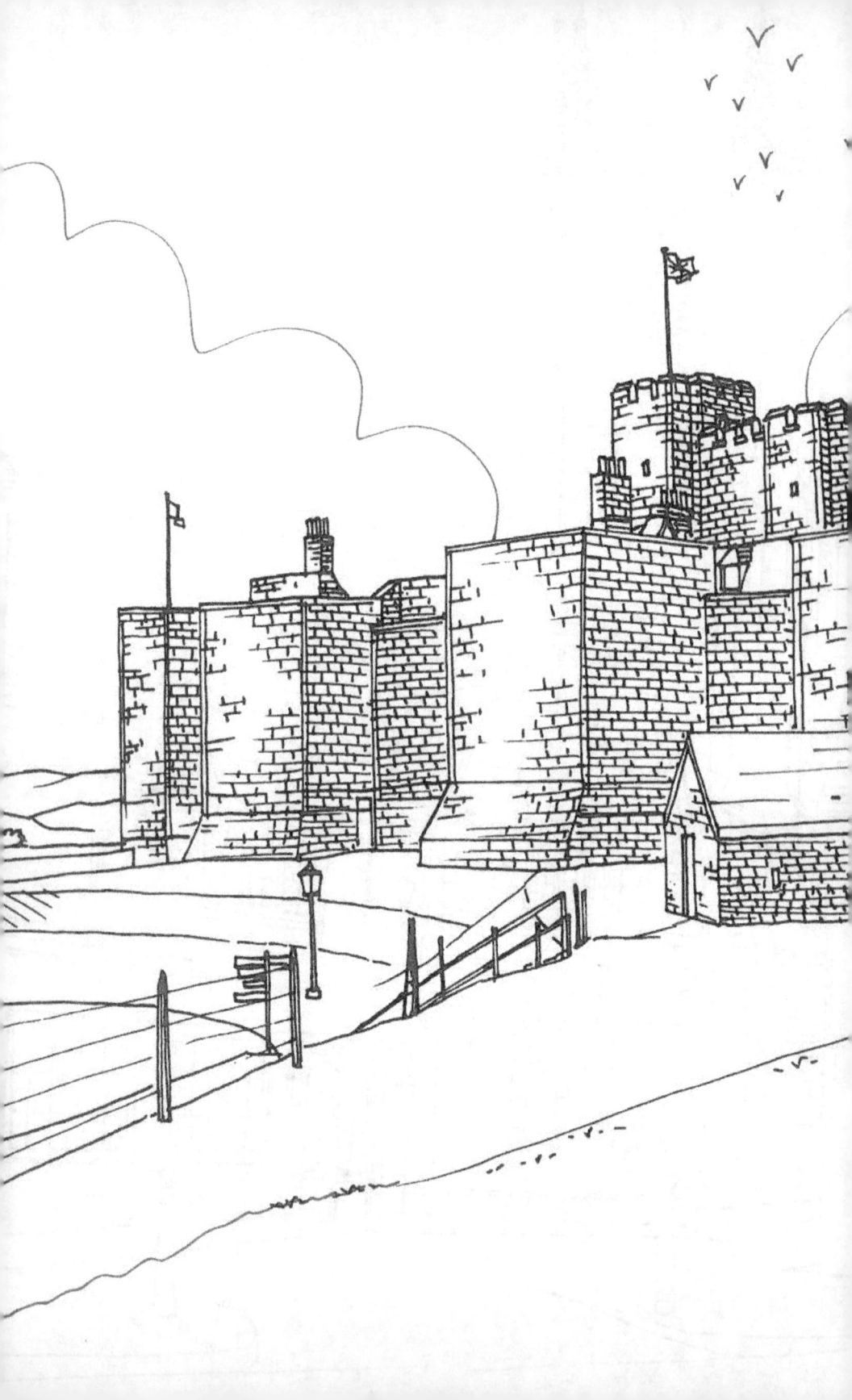

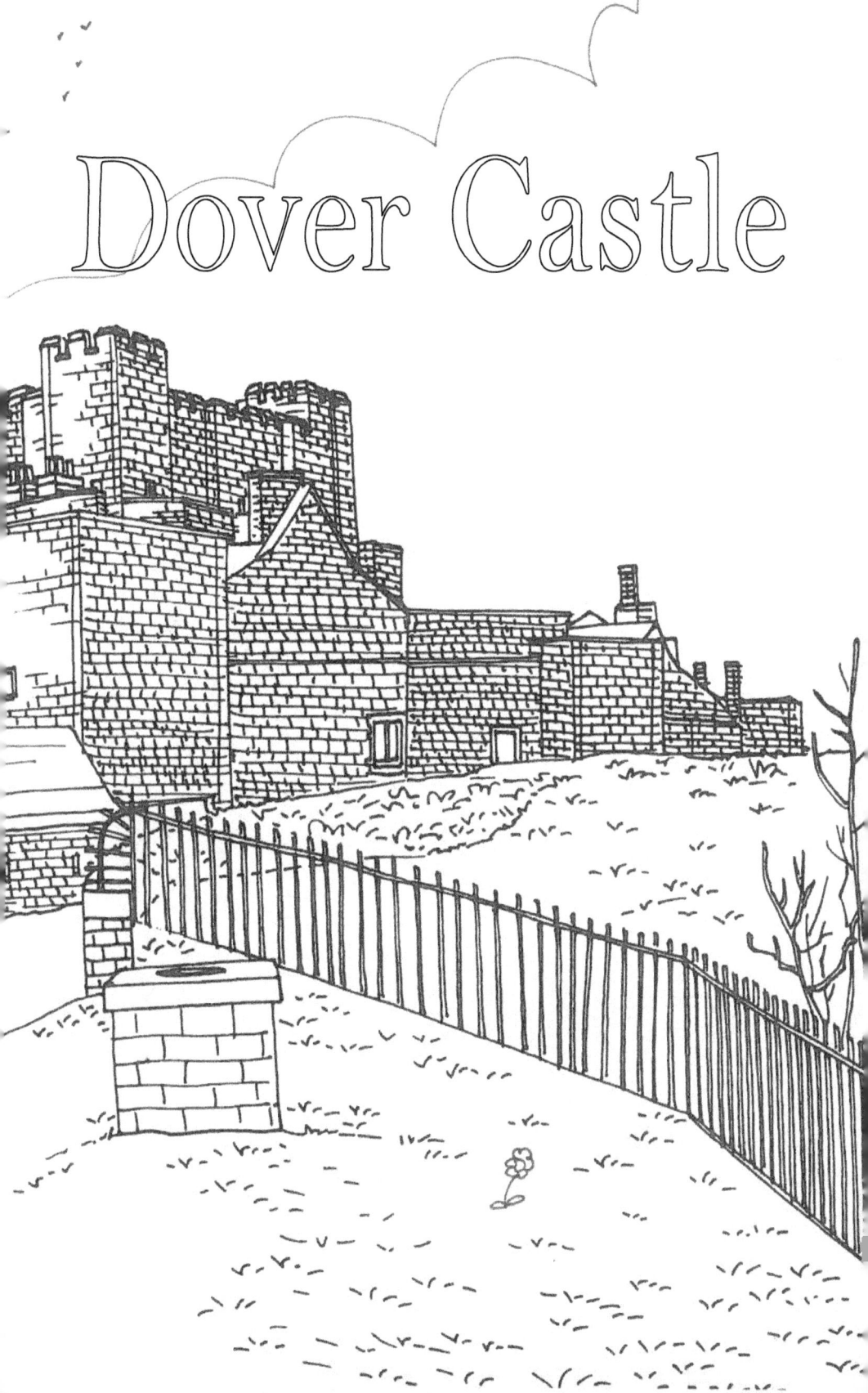

Dover Castle

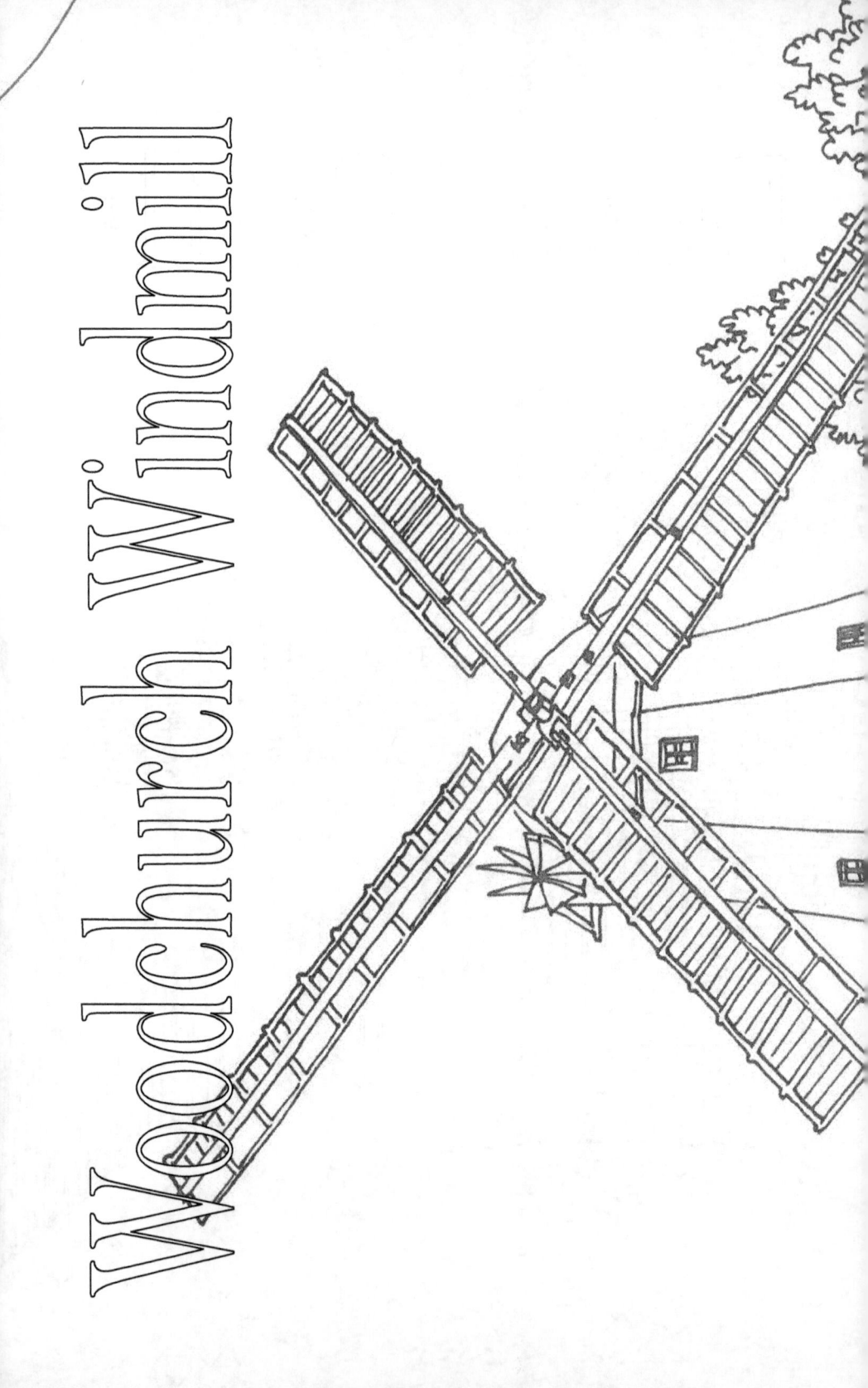

Woodchurch Windmill

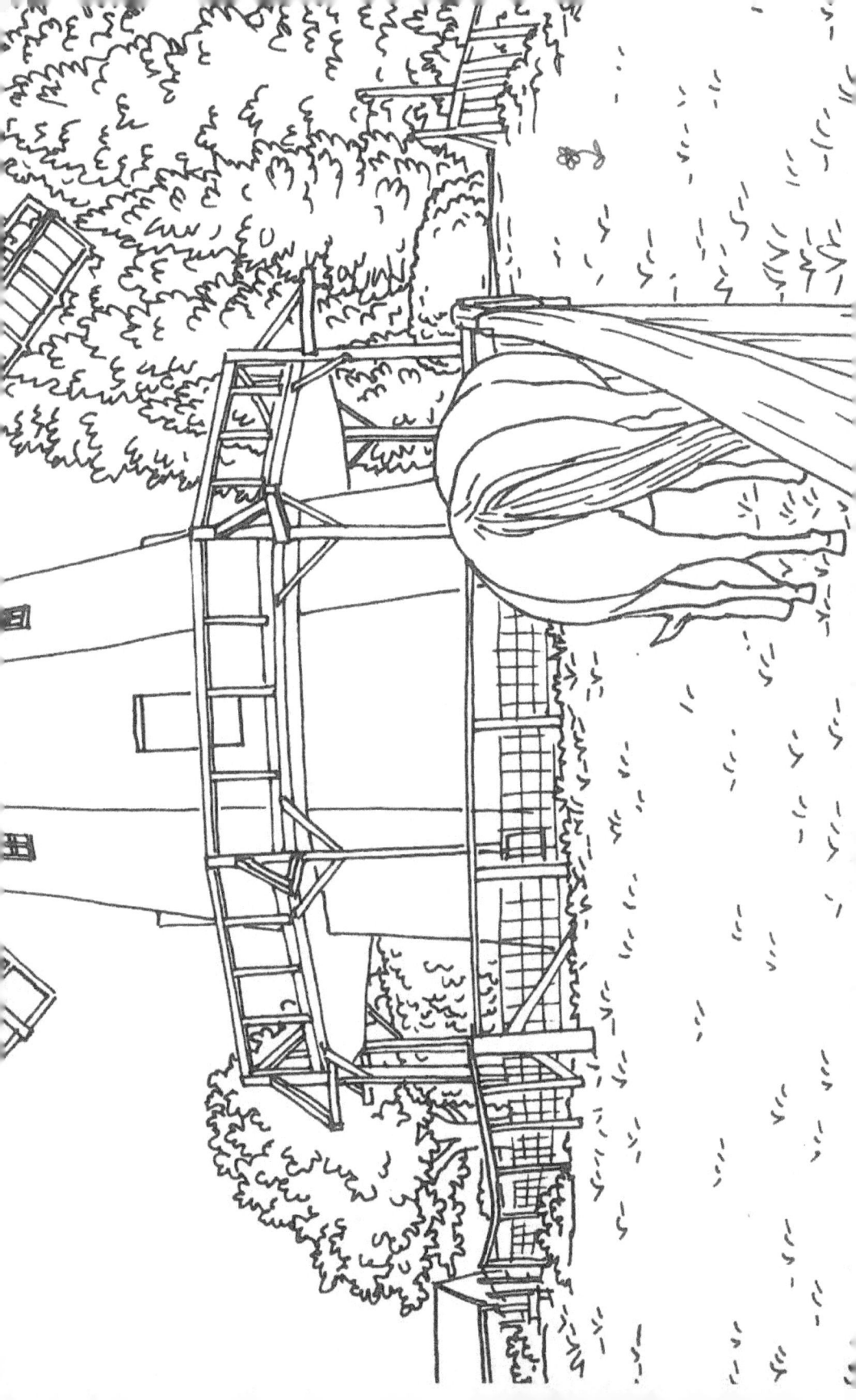

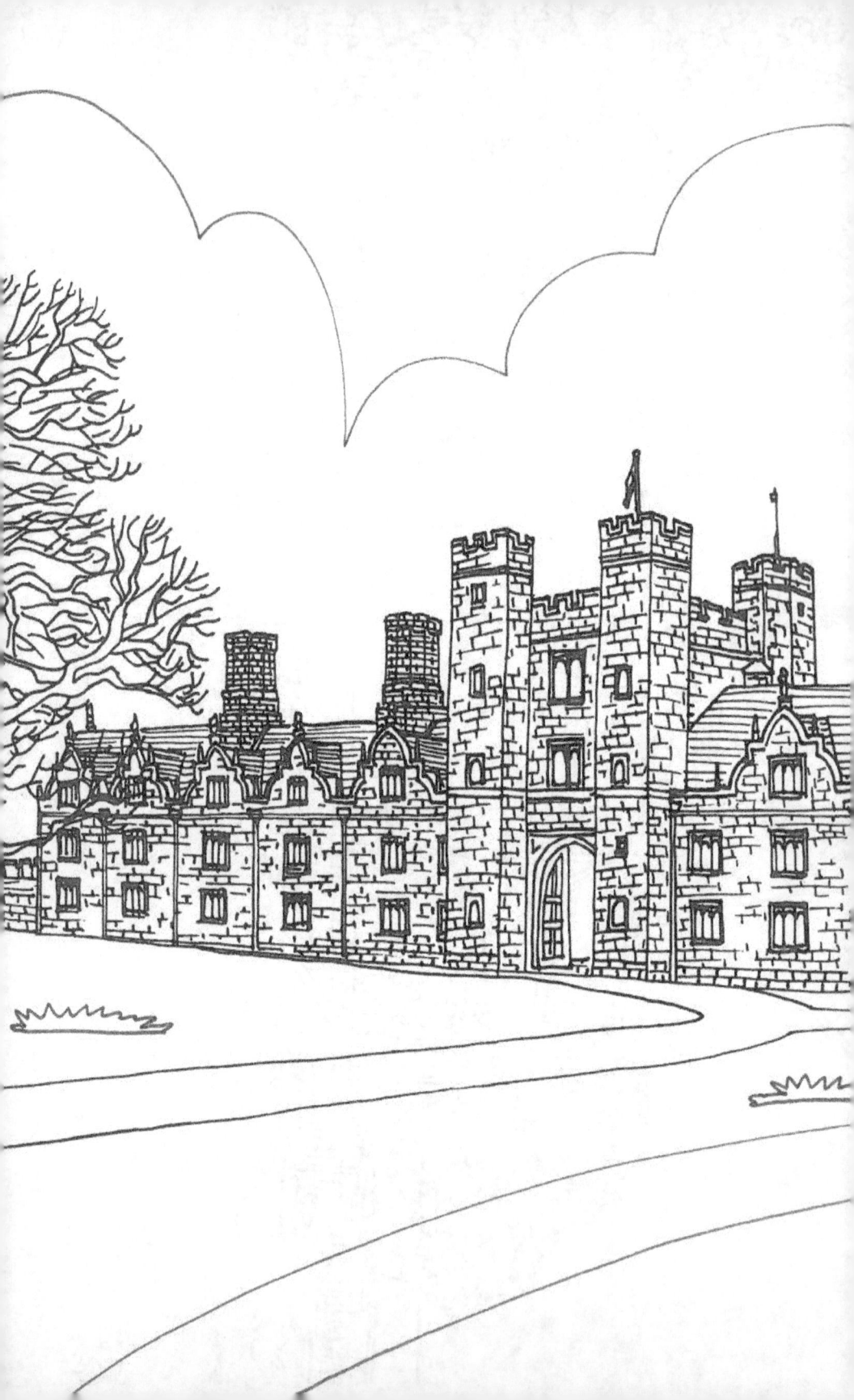

Knole House

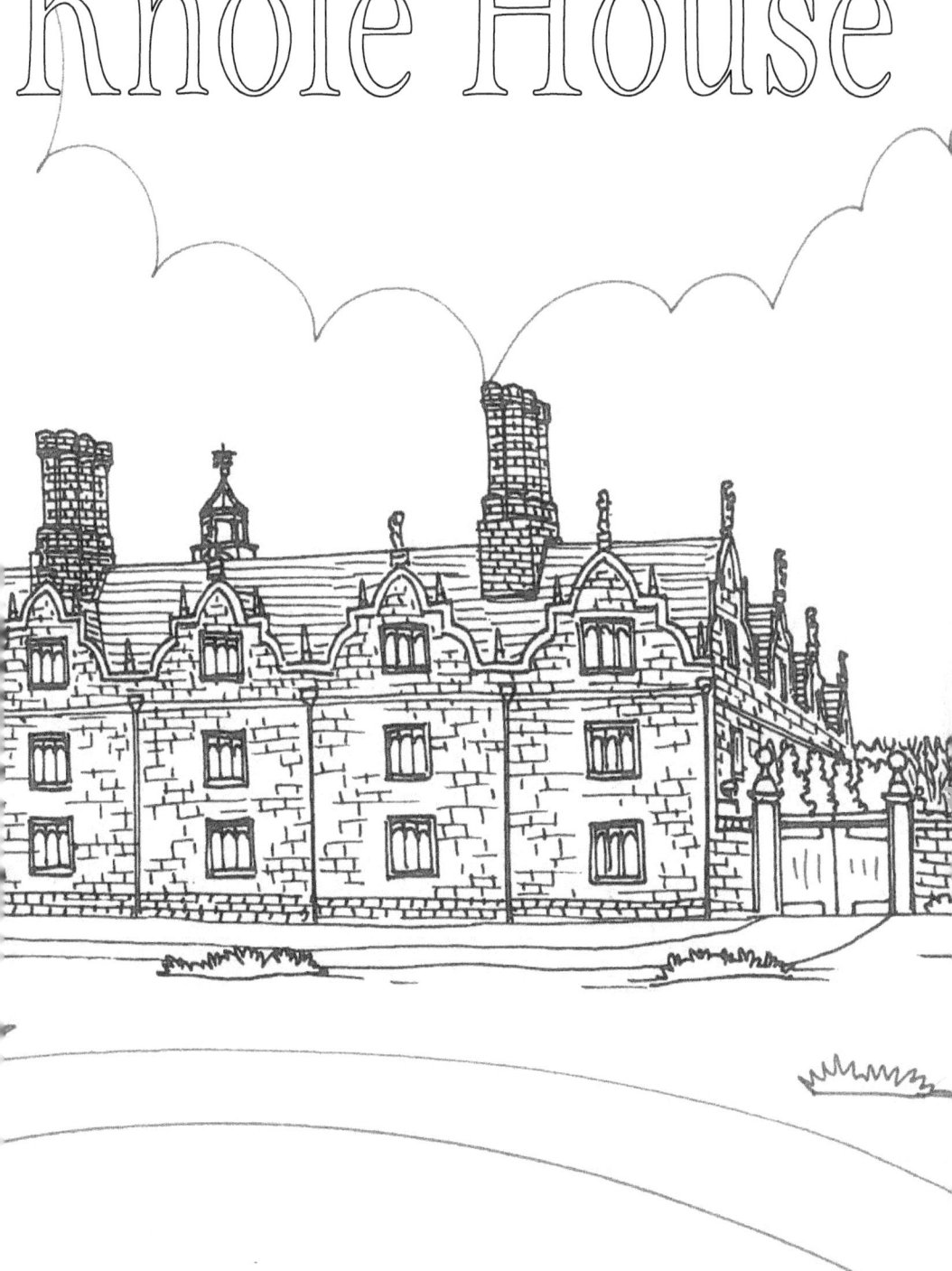

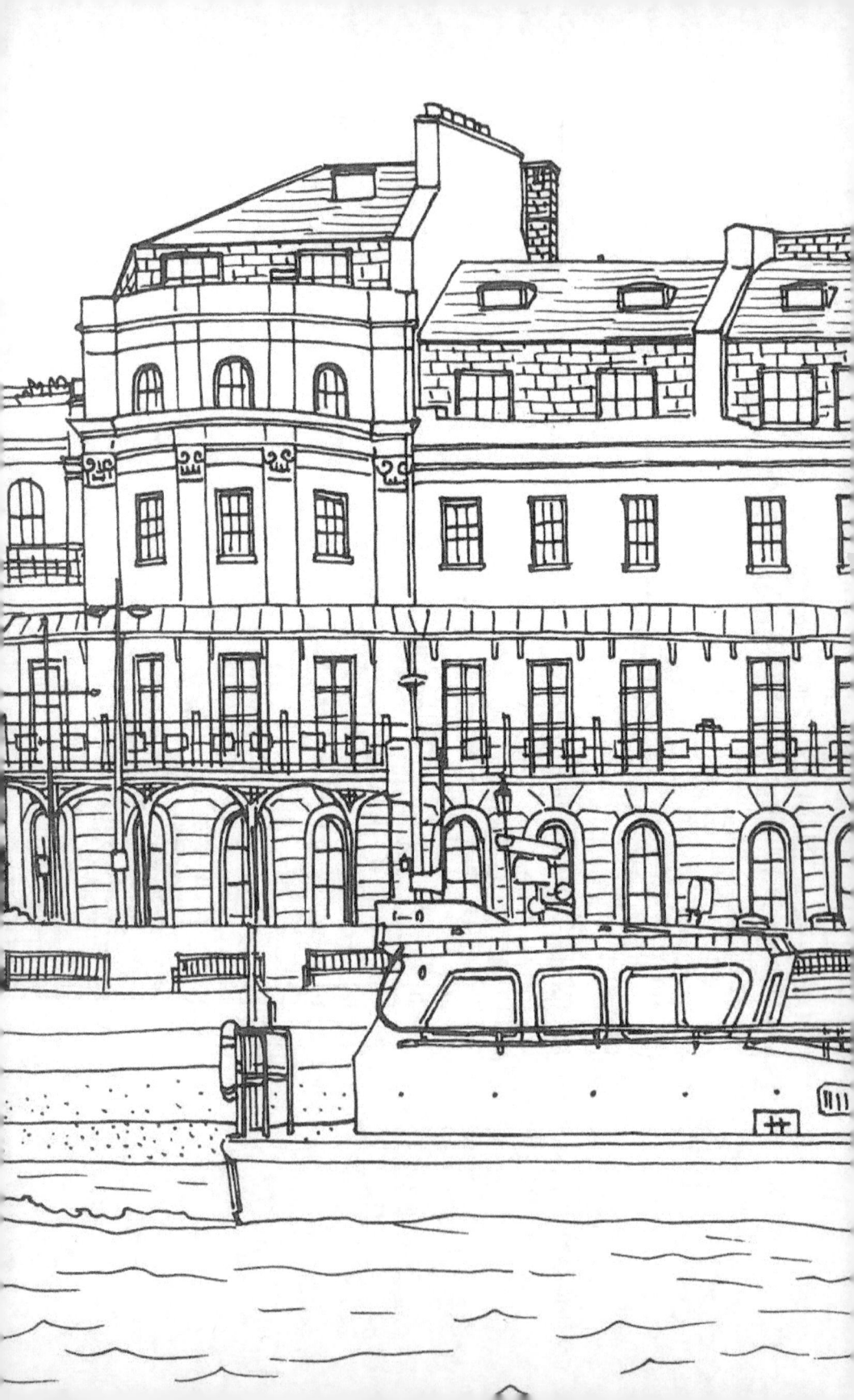

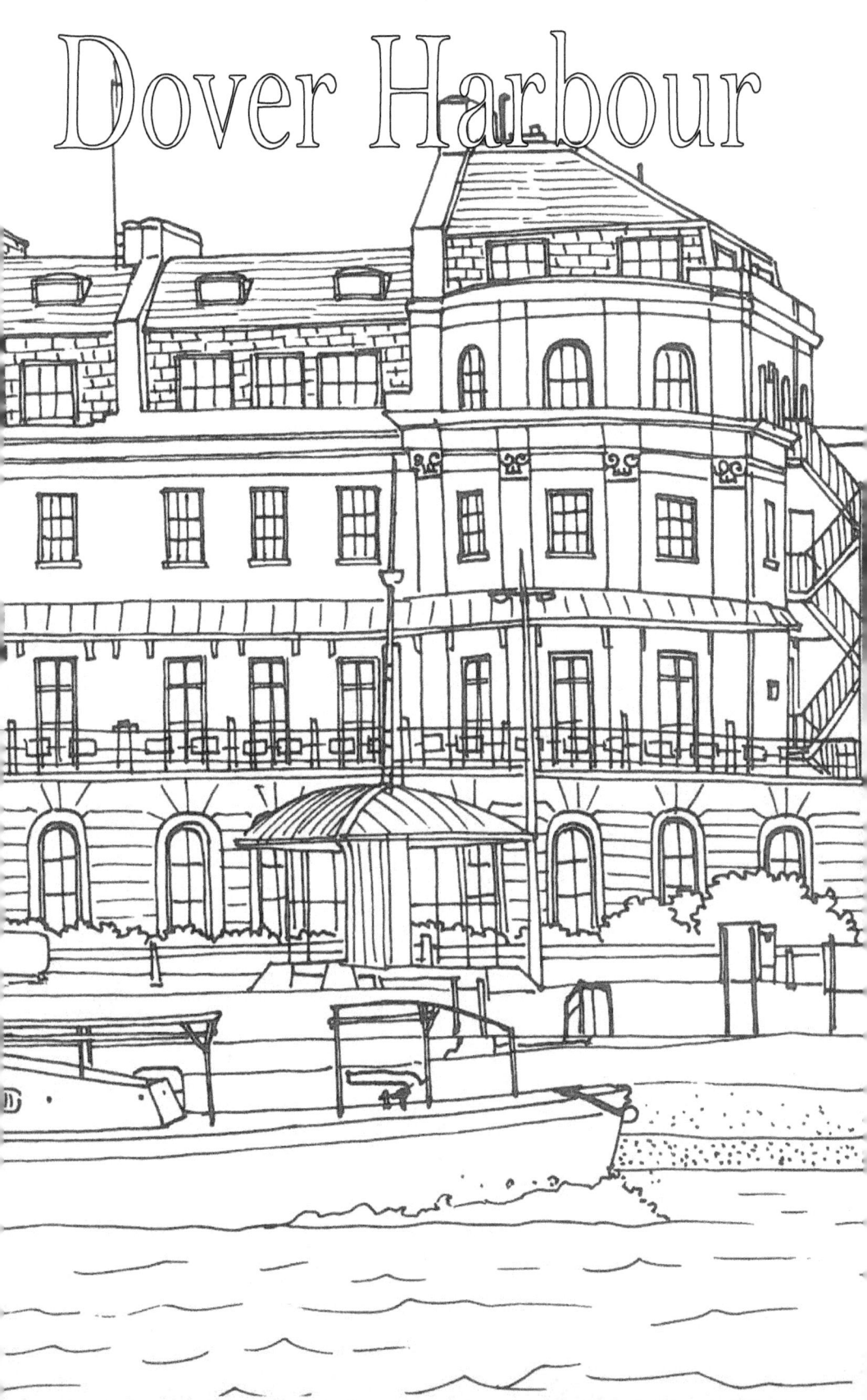

Dover Harbour

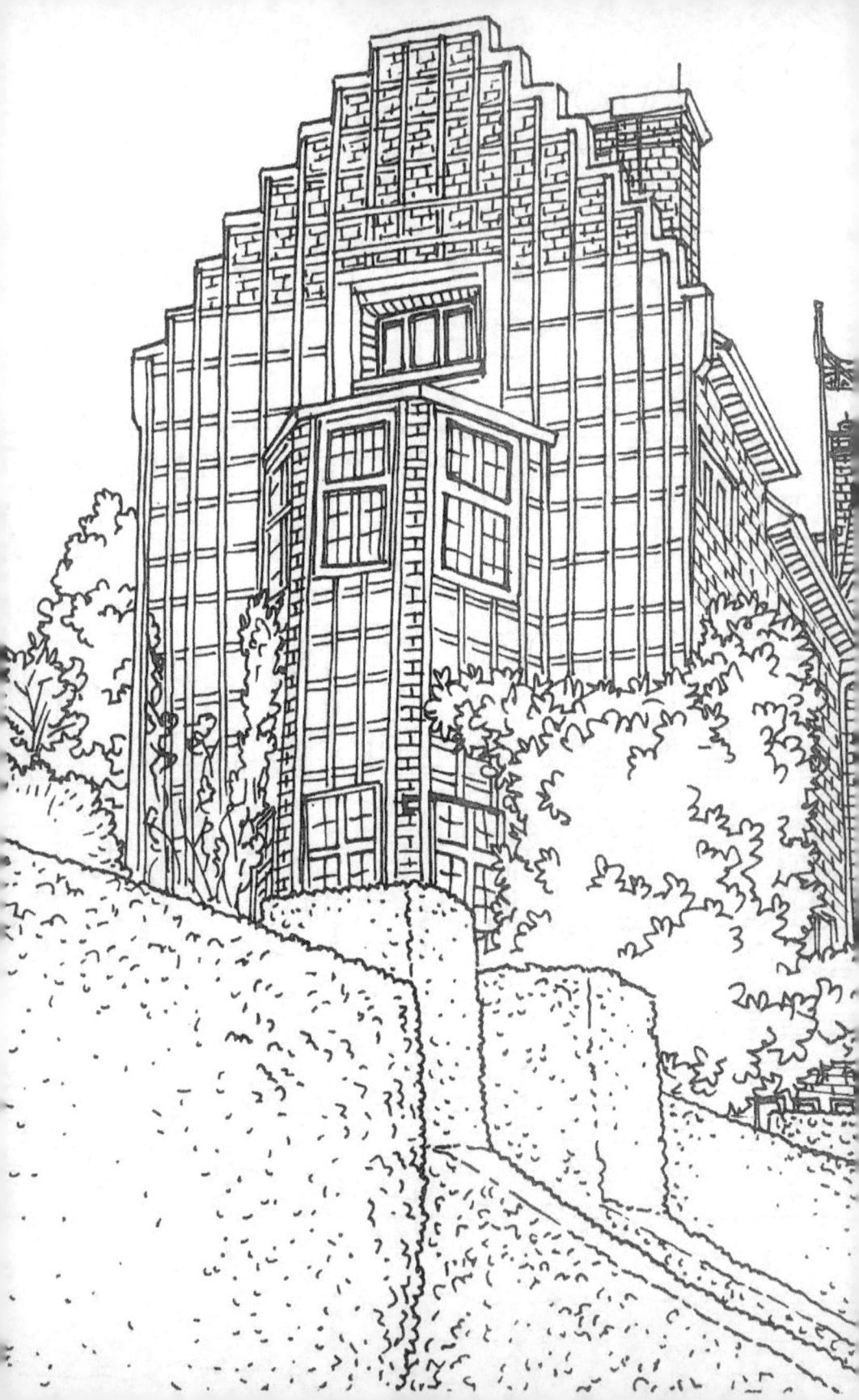

Chartwell House

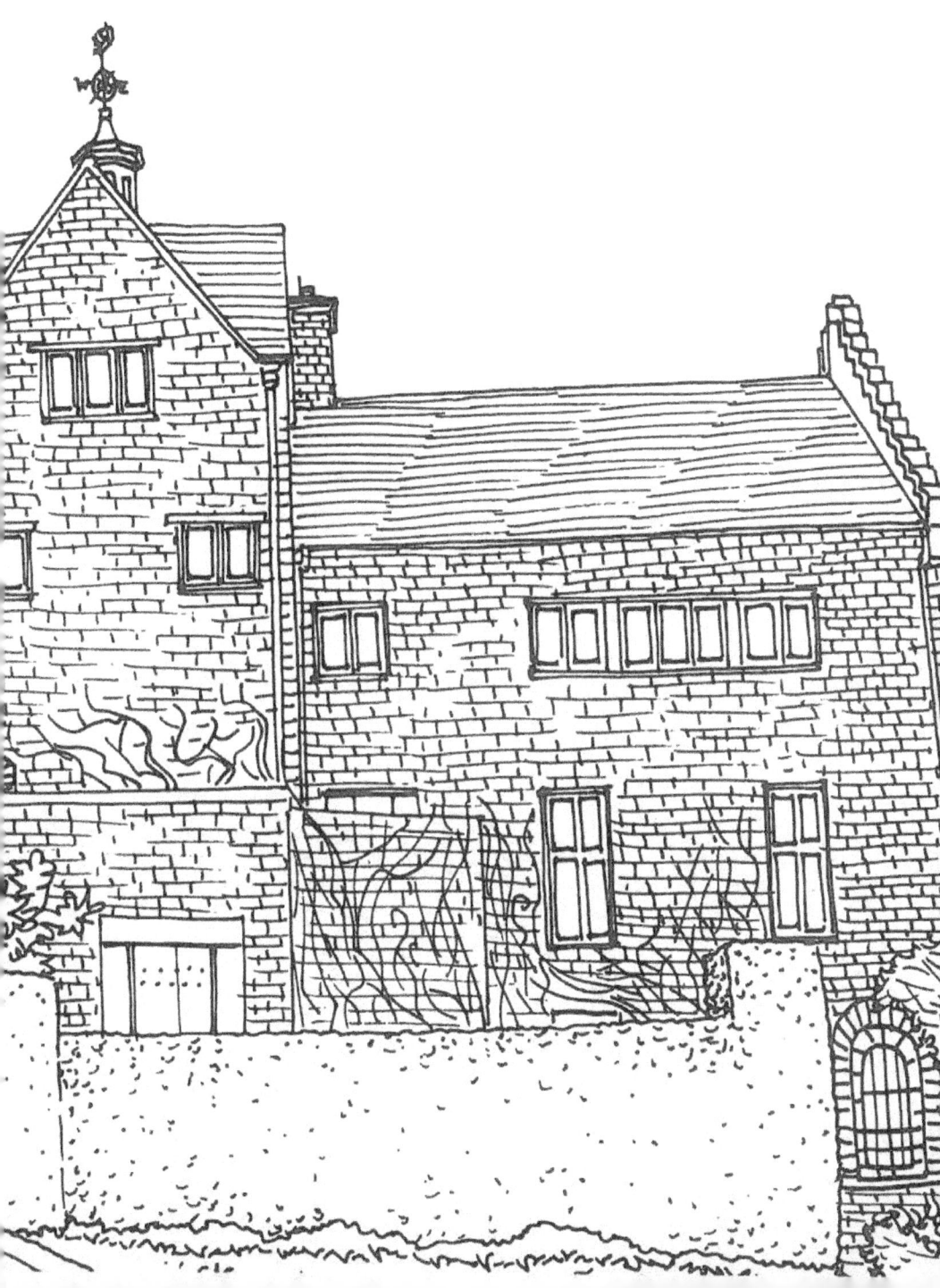

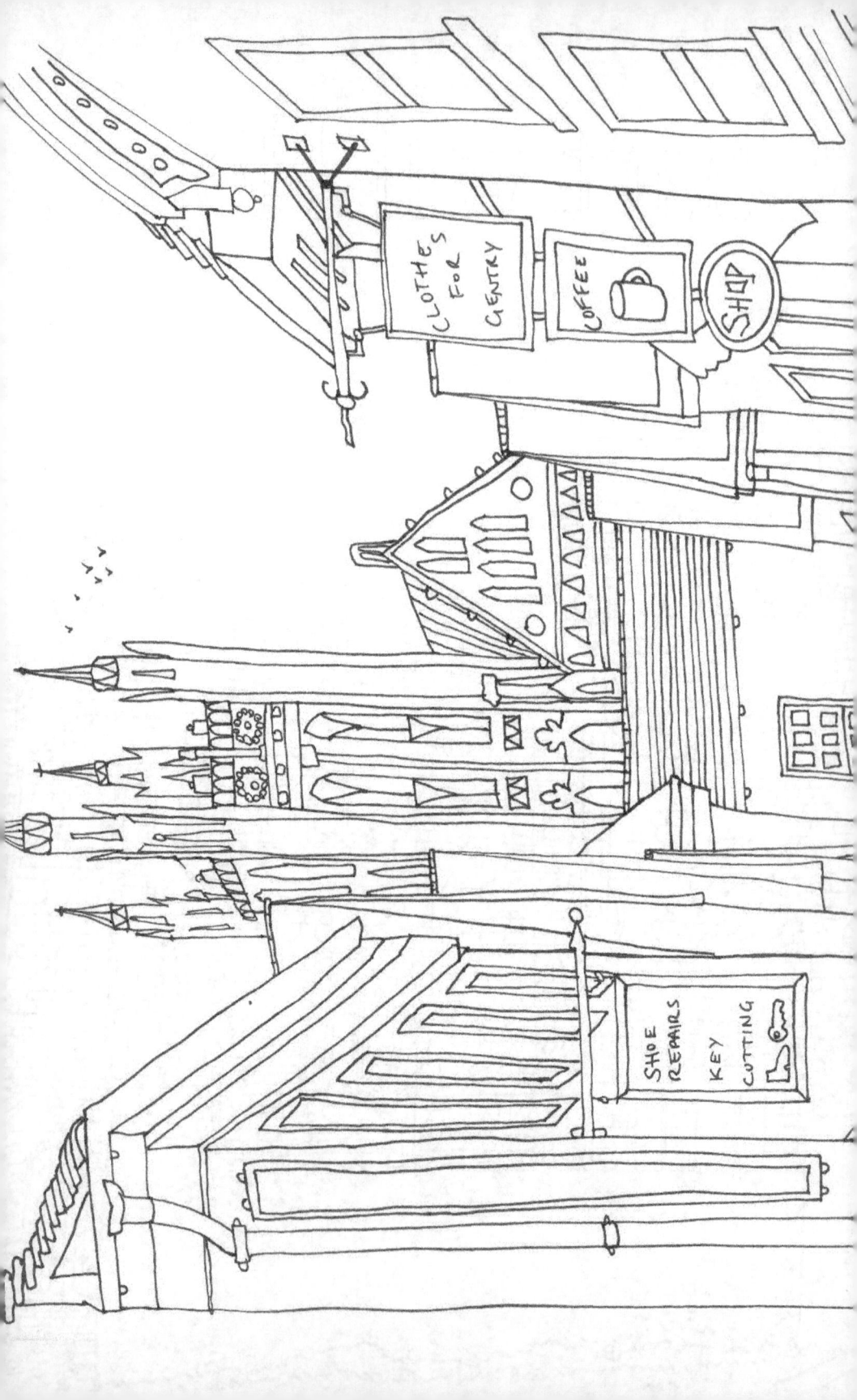

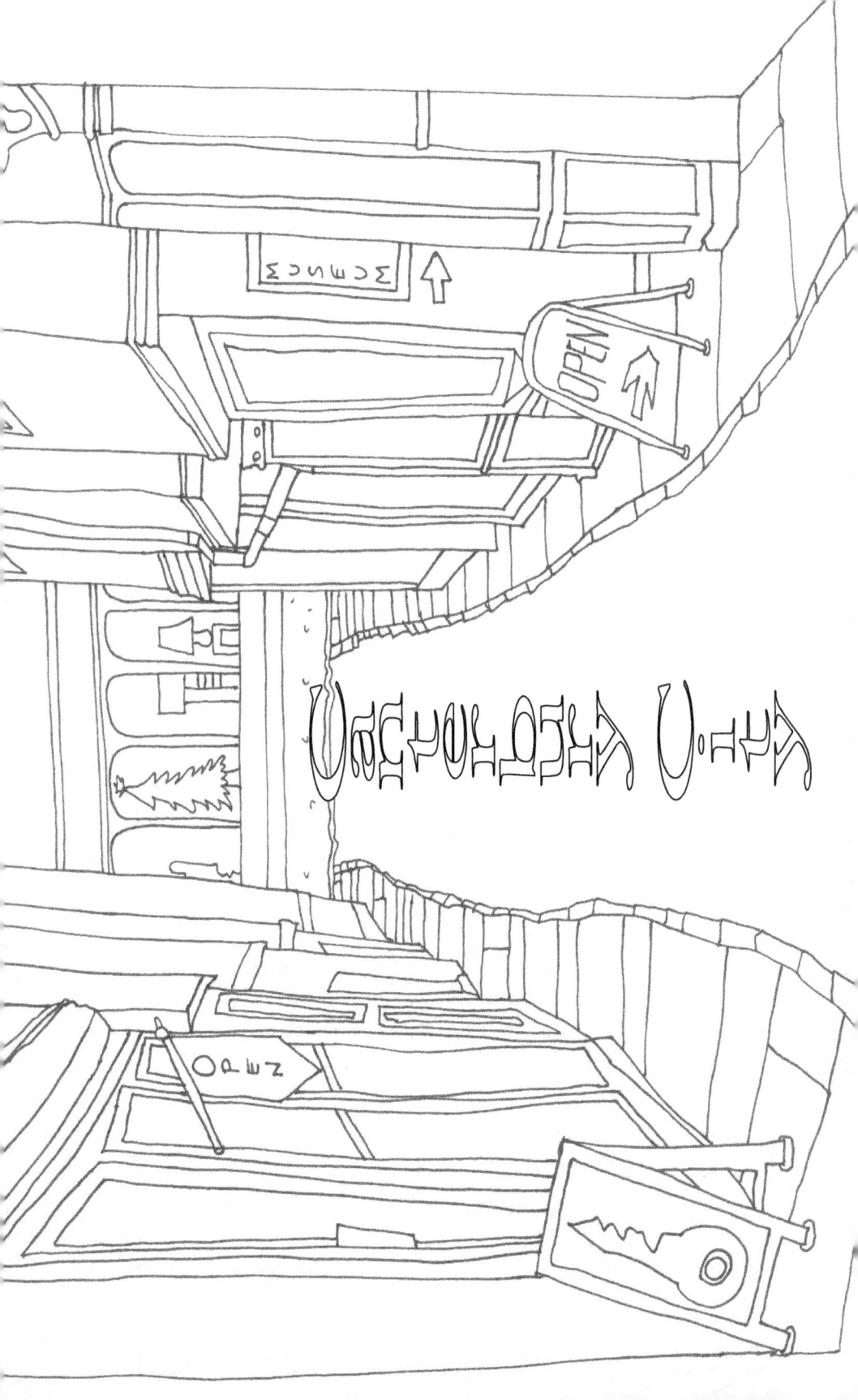

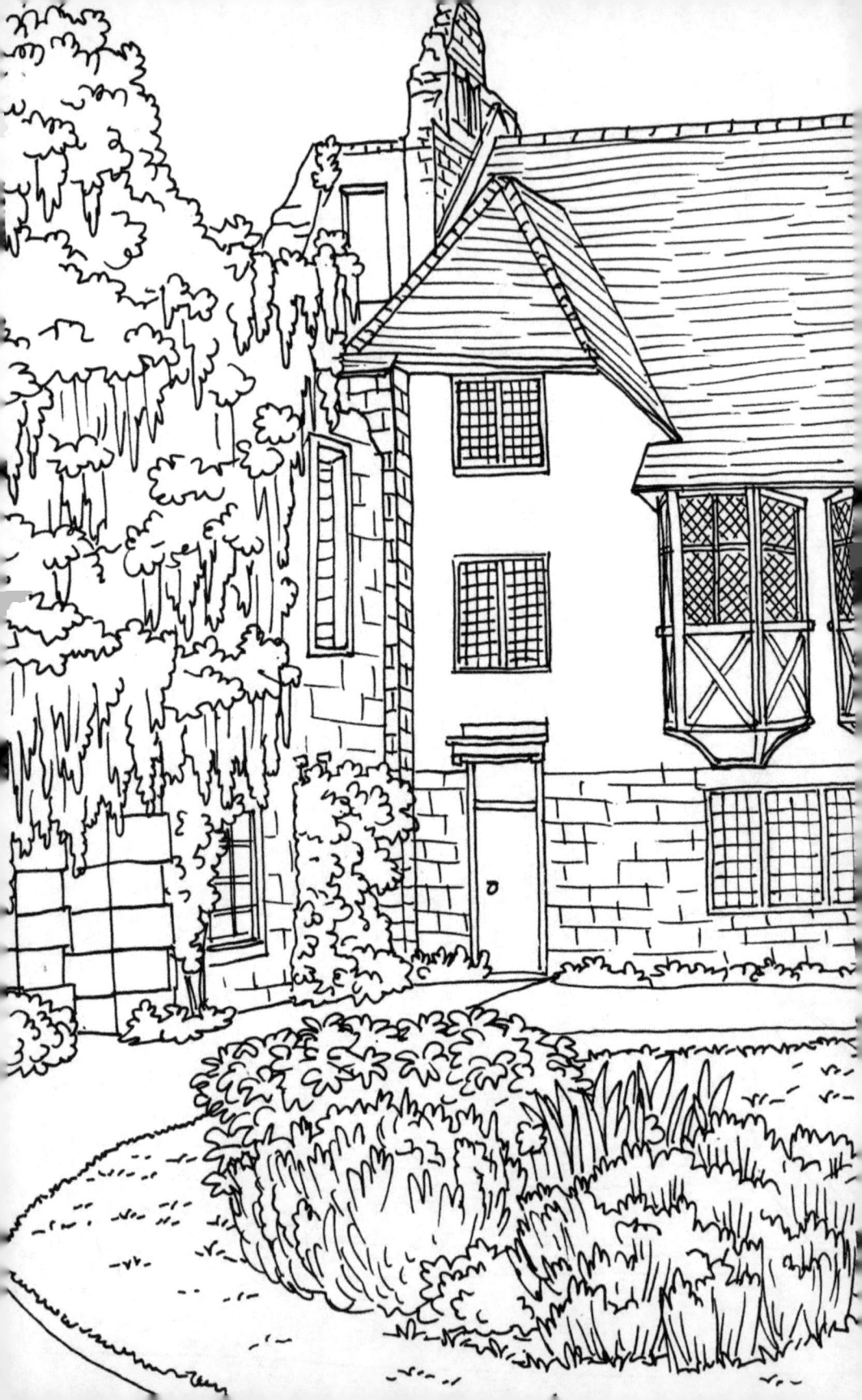

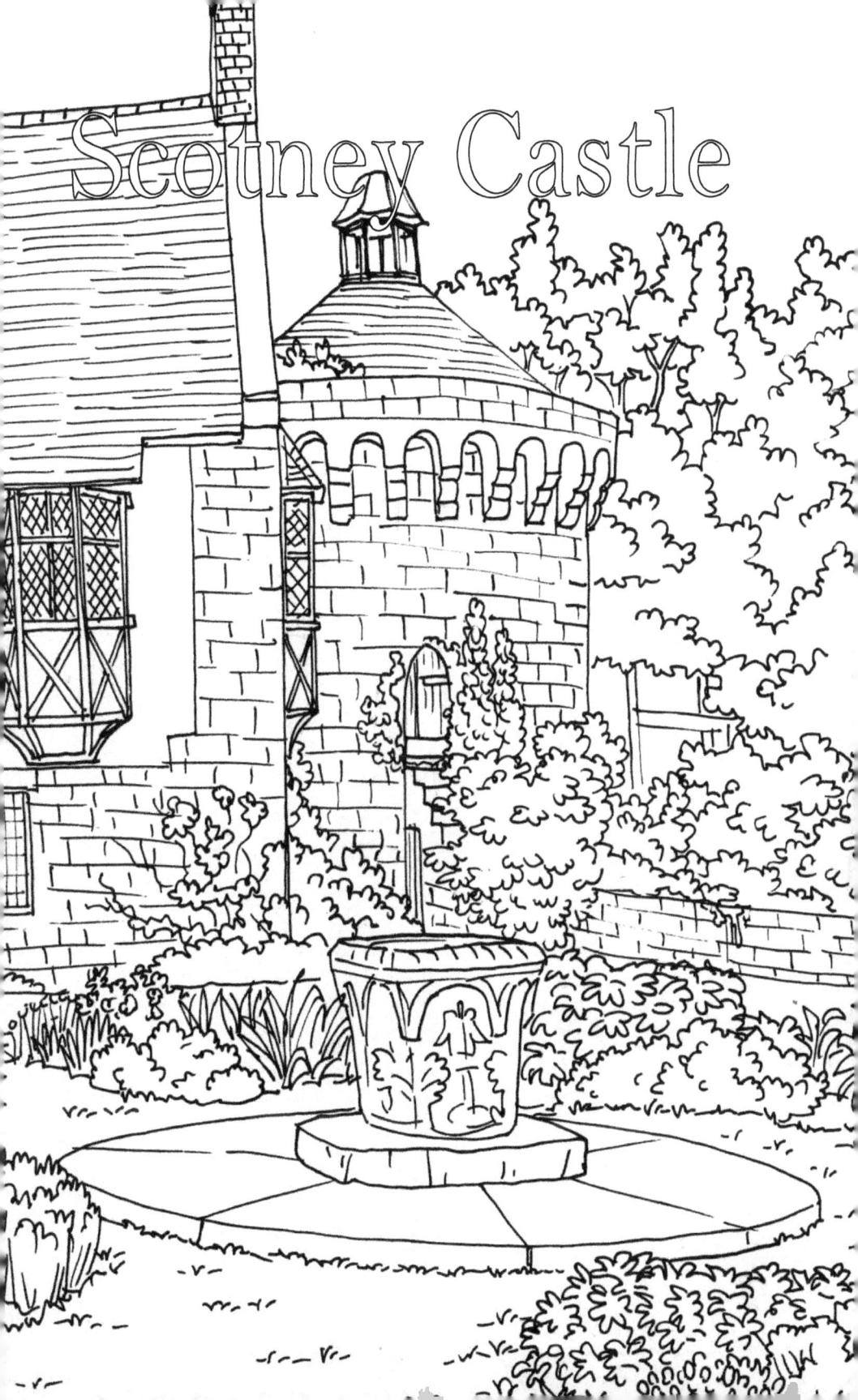

Scotney Castle

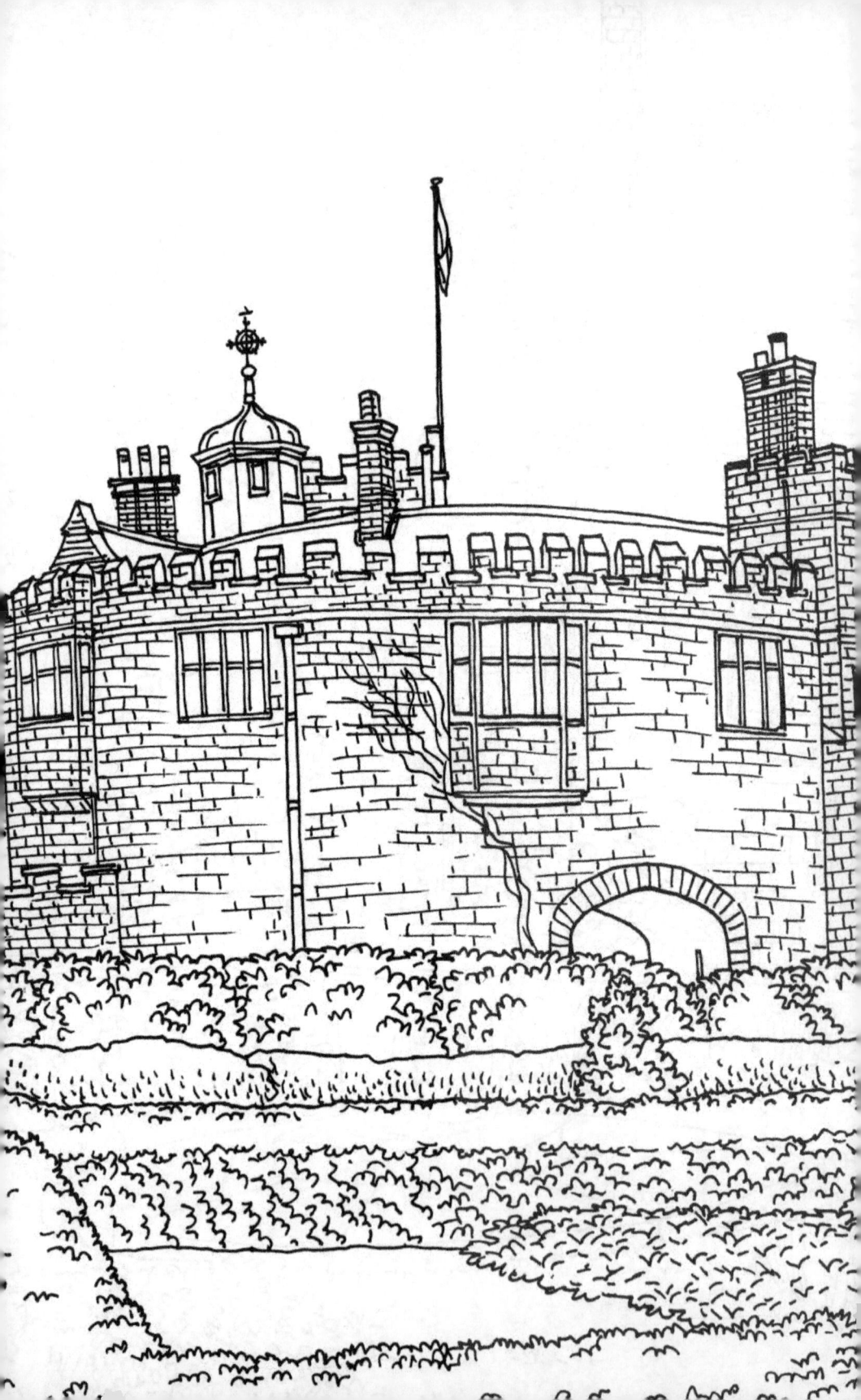

Walmer Castle & Gardens

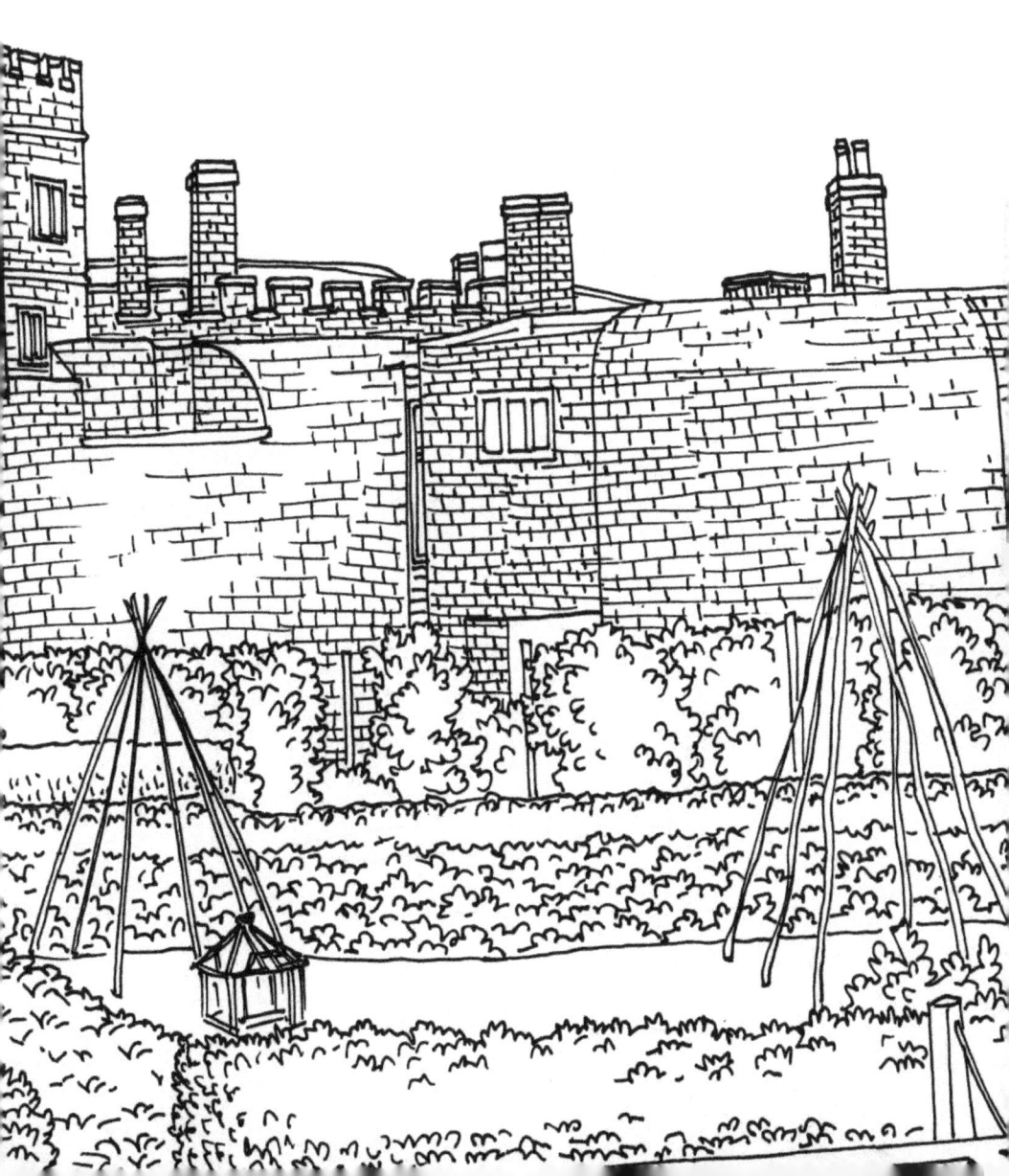

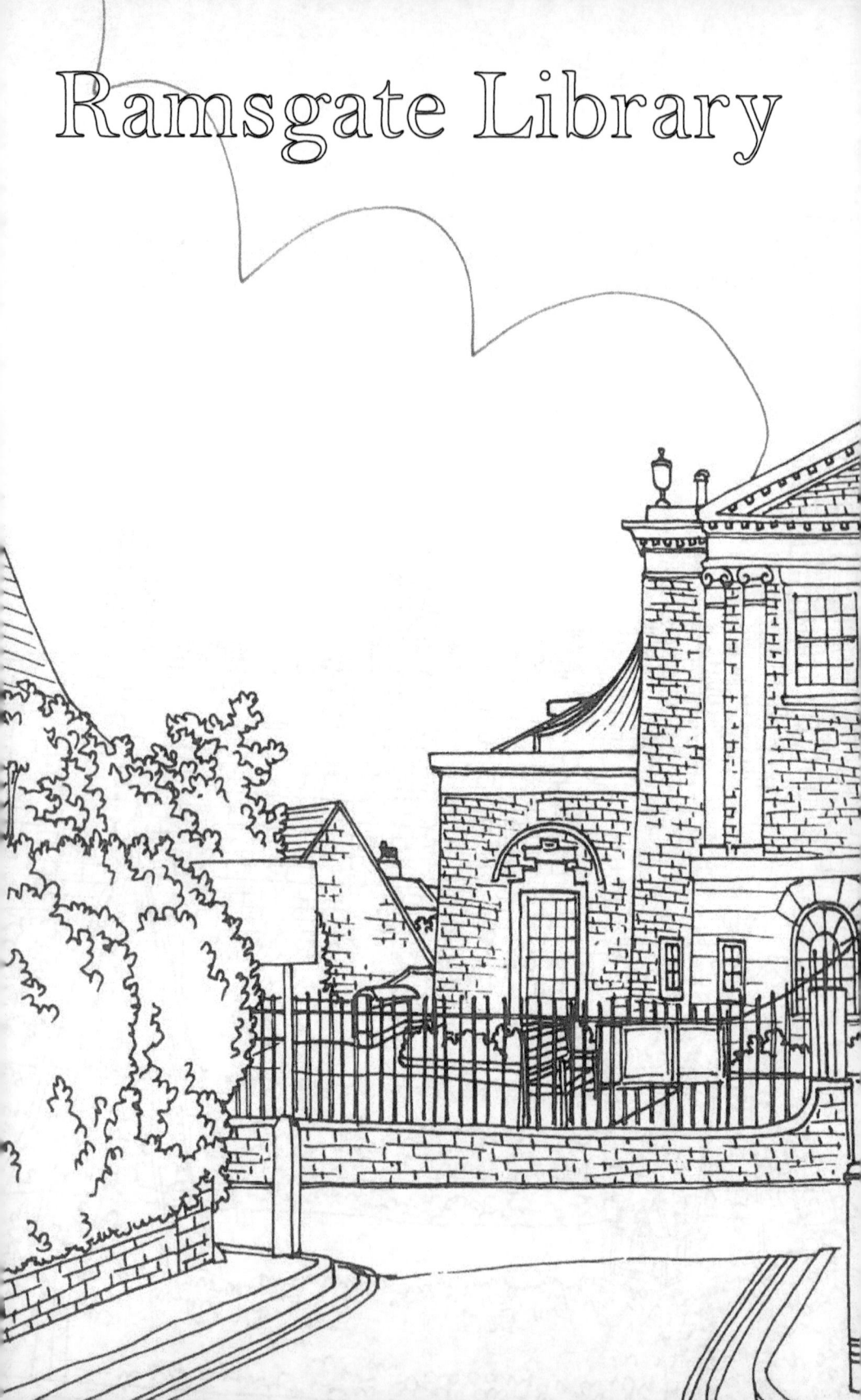

Ramsgate Library

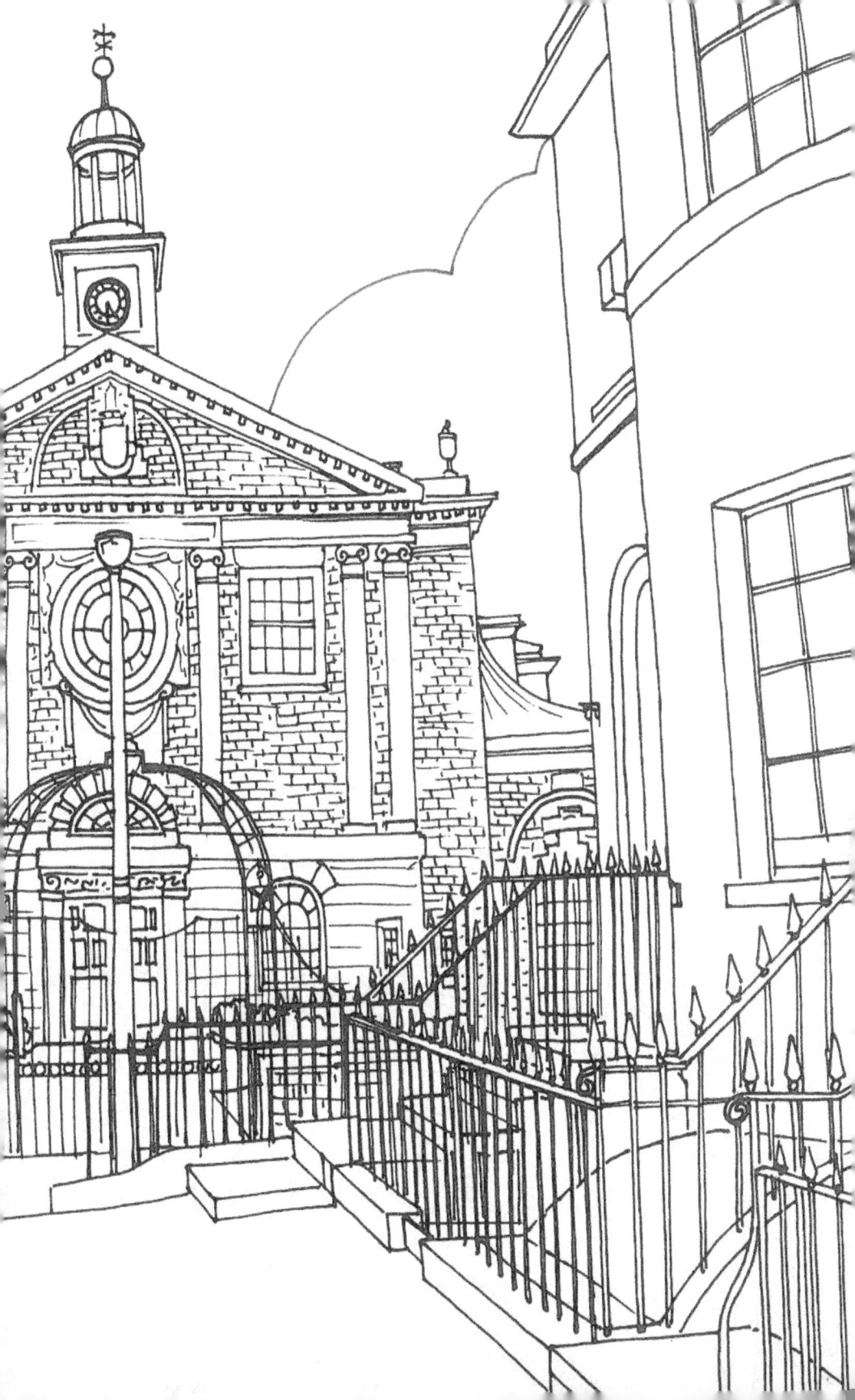

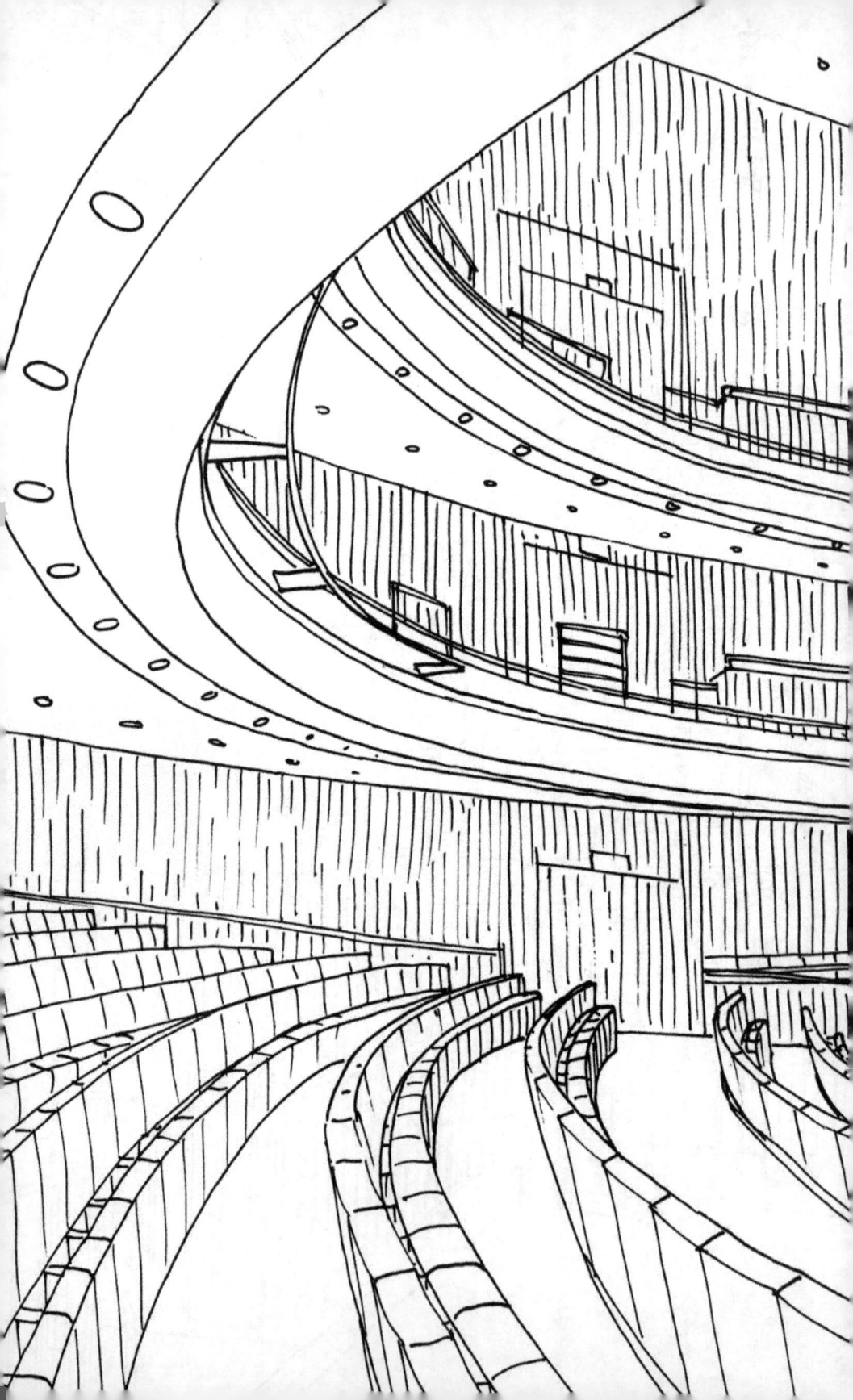

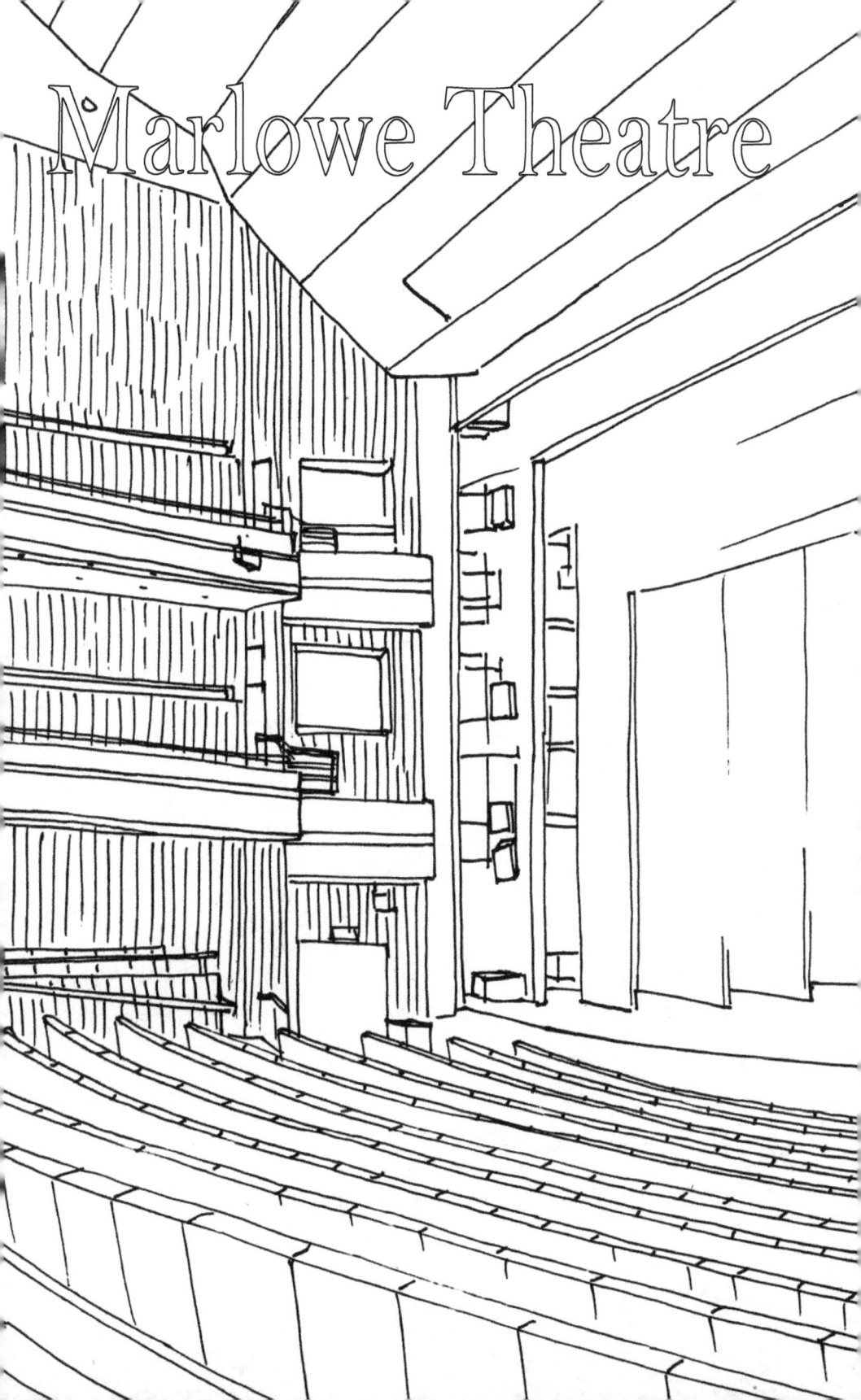

Ashford International
Rail Station

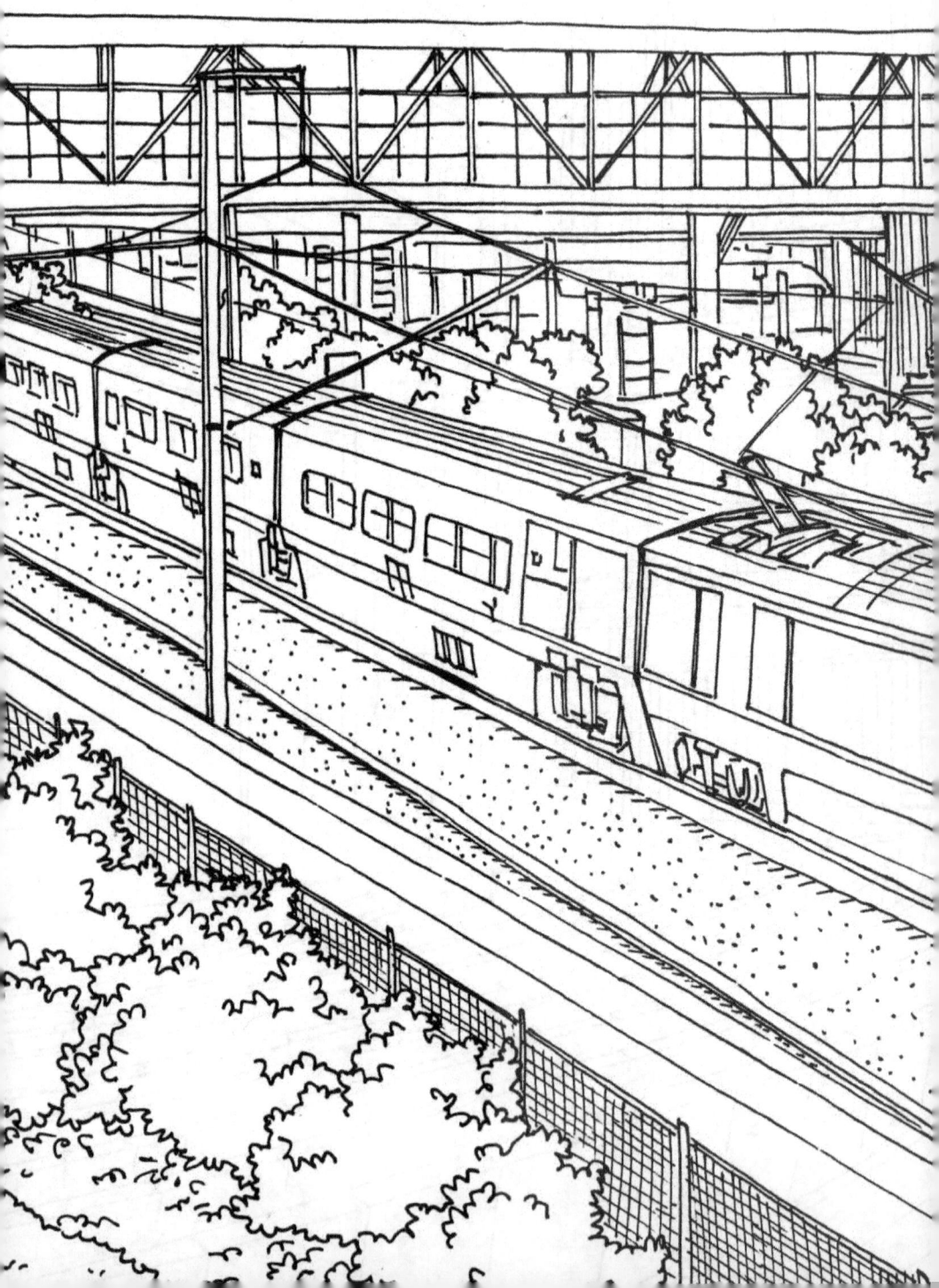

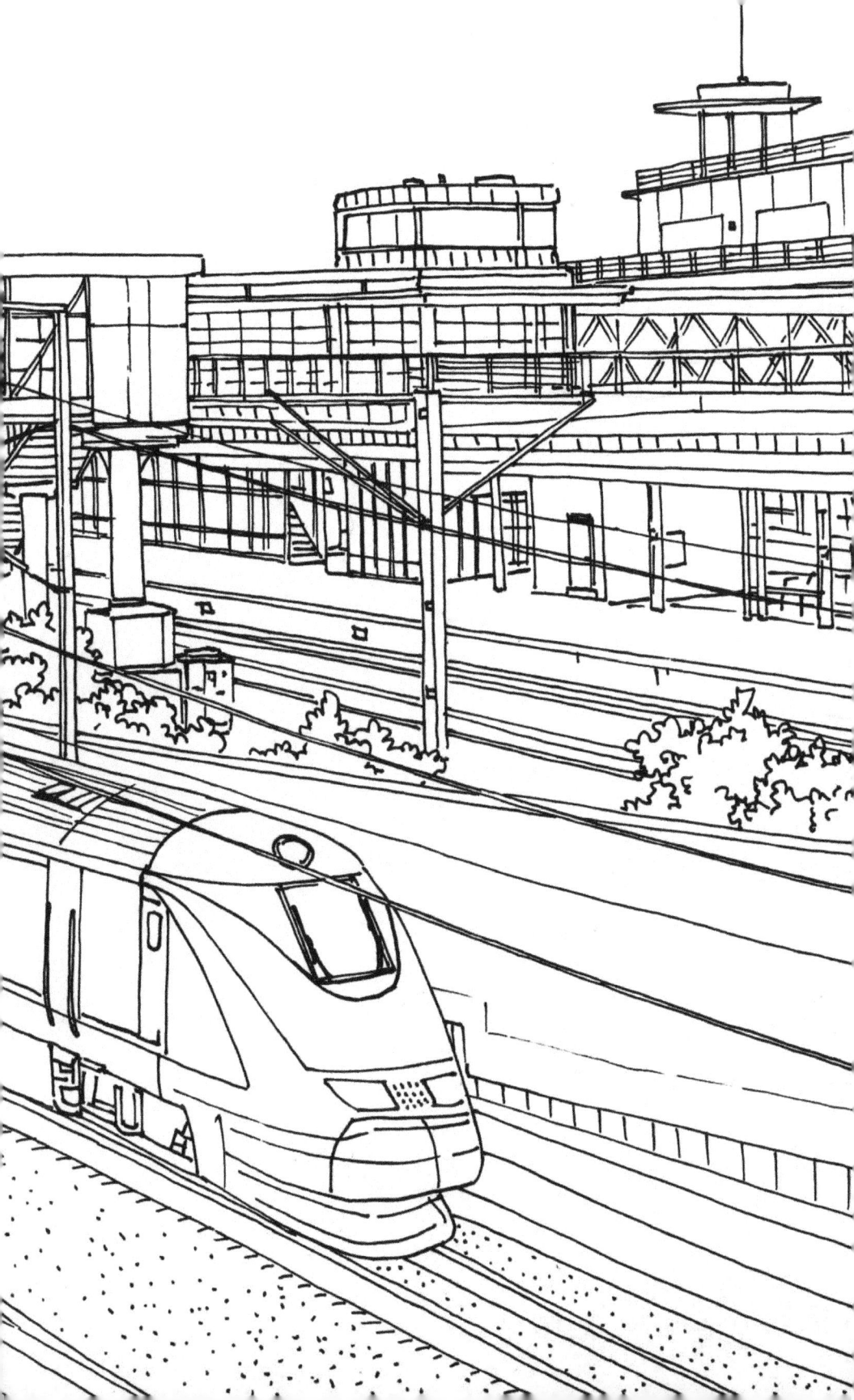